Point & Click Linux!

Your Guide to Trouble-Free Computing

Robin 'Roblimo' Miller

PRENTICE
HALL
PTR

An Imprint of PEARSON EDUCATION
Indianapolis, Indiana
www.phptr.com

Publisher: John Wait
Editor in Chief: Don O'Hagan
Publishing Partner: Mark L. Taub
Editorial Assistant: Noreen Regina
Marketing Manager: Robin O'Brien
Publicist: Heather Fox
Cover Designer: Anthony Gemmellaro
Managing Editor: Gina Kanouse
Senior Project Editor: Kristy Hart
Production: Specialized Composition, Inc.
Interior Designer: Kim Scott
Manufacturing Buyer: Dan Uhrig

 2005 Pearson Education, Inc.
Publishing as Prentice Hall Professional Technical Reference
Upper Saddle River, New Jersey 07458

The publisher offers excellent discounts on this book when ordered in quantity for bulk purchases or special sales, which may include electronic versions and/or custom covers and content particular to your business, training goals, marketing focus, and branding interests. For more information, please contact:

U. S. Corporate and Government Sales
(800) 382-3419
corpsales@pearsontechgroup.com

For sales outside the U. S., please contact:

International Sales
international@pearsoned.com

Visit us on the Web: www.phptr.com

Library of Congress Cataloging-in-Publication Data:

2004110315

Table of Contents

Section III Beyond the Basics

Appendices

Acknowledgments

A large number of people did most of the "real work" that made this book possible, notably thousands of Linux, GNU, KDE, Debian, and other free and open source software developers. It's impossible to thank each one individually here; the list of names and accomplishments would take many hundreds of pages.

Warren Woodford and the MEPIS development team created the *SimplyMEPIS* CD in the back of this book; they also maintain the MEPIS.org/forum Web site that is the primary source of technical support for MEPIS Linux. Please consider supporting their work by registering your copy at MEPIS.org or—better yet—purchasing a MEPIS subscription. The price is small and the benefits are large.

Jem Matzan and Joe Barr contributed chapters and helped me make sure the manuscript had as few technical errors as possible. Howard Lee Harkness and Jay Lyman also contributed valuable suggestions, as did many visitors to PointAndClickLinux.com who commented on early chapters I posted there while the book was still taking shape.

The PointAndClickLinux.com Web site was created by Brice Burgess; Damen Shaquiri of EvolvMedia made the video DVD. Logan Tygart and other members of the Suncoast Linux Users Group helped develop the VNC-based production method we used for the videos, a project that has now taken on a life of its own beyond this book. (You can see some of this work in the form of additional videos available at PointAndClickLinux.com.)

Elise Walter had the unenviable task of whipping the final manuscript into publishable form. I am a cantankerous and often quirky writer, but she remained patient with me and got the job done—and done well.

And when it comes to patience, my wife Debbie is the reigning world champion. My normal workweek as editor in chief for a group of open source news and information Web sites (OSTG.com) is draining enough; when I piled the work of turning out a book on deadline on top of that, Debbie hardly had a husband for many months. She literally brought me meals in my home office and rubbed my shoulders as I typed late into the night. I have never understood why such a beautiful, talented, and supportive woman chose to marry me, but I am not complaining. Instead, I am showering her with gifts, hugs, and everything else I can think of in return for her help in making this book possible.

-Robin 'Roblimo' Miller
Bradenton, Florida

About the Author

 **Robin "Roblimo" Miller** started writing professionally in 1983 as a free-lance reporter and feature writer in Baltimore, Maryland. He first wrote about Linux in 1997, and by 1998 he was a full-time Linux user, working as a reporter, columnist, and editor for Andover News Network, which later become the OSTG (Open Source Technology Group) division of VA Software.

Roblimo, as he has been known online since the mid-1990s, was one of the first reporters to cover the Linux phenomenon. He has spoken at computing and Internet conferences in Saudi Arabia, Mexico, India, Trinidad, Jordan, and at least a dozen U.S. states. He's been "the computer expert" for the award-winning *Rise and Shine* morning show on Baltimore's WJZ TV, and has been a guest on many radio and several cable TV talk shows.

Point & Click Linux! is Roblimo's second book. His first, The *Online Rules of Successful Companies*, was published by FT Prentice Hall in 2002. He has written over 2000 articles for various newspapers, magazines, and Web sites on topics including Linux (of course!), child support, college campus drug use, metallurgy, magnetic resonance imaging (MRI), software development, telemarketing, crime prevention, tax policy, online business, TV news reporting, taxi driving, and political shenanigans.

Before becoming a full-time writer and editor, Roblimo worked as a limo owner/driver (hence "Roblimo"), taxi driver, electronics technician, soldier, and auto mechanic. He is currently editor in chief of OSTG, and lives with his wife, the artist Deborah Miller, in Bradenton, Florida.

Foreword

You should be using Linux for the same reason I eat brown eggs.

A century ago, chicken eggs came in all sorts of colors: brown, green, blue, and red, but in the past few decades, consumer demand for white eggs has nearly eliminated breeds of chickens that lay other colors. Ninety percent of all eggs in the U.S. are laid by white leghorns. Experts say this homogenization of the chicken gene threatens the health, and ultimately the survival, of the species.

Does that sound bananas? It's not. In fact, it's exactly what has happened to bananas. Inbreeding has drained the gene pool and weakened the fruit's resistance to disease. As a result the banana as we know it may become extinct in just a decade. What does all this have to do with computer operating systems? Everything.

The nearly total dominance of Microsoft Windows is the technological equivalent of white eggs and bananas. A few more years of the Windows startup screen and you may not be able to boot anything else. And that's bad. Variety in technology has the same benefits as ecological variety: competition breeds better birds; variety sparks innovation. It also keeps prices down, slows down hackers, and gives you a choice. You may not choose to use Linux, but it's good to have the choice. And as Robin will show you in this book, it's a great choice for most of us.

People usually first consider Linux because of its price. You can't beat free. Eventually they realize there are even better reasons to use Linux. Many large companies use it for its reliability. Others like the speed with which security patches and updates are released. Some prefer Linux because they can modify and improve the operating system and its accompanying programs by themselves. Lately many Windows users who are fed up with viruses and spyware have chosen Linux as a safe haven from these information super-highwaymen. These are all excellent reasons. But now you know that it's also good public policy to support Linux. Linux is good for everyone, even people who still use Windows. The mere fact that Linux exists forces Microsoft to make a better product, keep prices low, and puts pressure on them to take security and reliability seriously. If you think Windows is getting better, thank a Linux user. If you don't think it's getting better, maybe you should *be* a Linux user.

But don't choose Linux just because it's good for you. Linux tastes great, too. Thanks to the efforts of thousands of programmers all over the world, Linux has evolved from an operating system for geeks into a computer system for the rest of us. (Sorry, Apple.)

Even if you've been using Microsoft Windows for years, you may be surprised at how easy it is to move to Linux. You'll have to retrain your brain a little, sure, but these days Linux works pretty much the way you'd expect. You'll already know how to do most of the things you want to do. And thanks to this book, it will be easy to figure out the rest. Don't worry that switching to Linux will narrow your choices, either. Linux can do everything but make an omelet. And I bet there's someone in a garage somewhere who's figuring out a way to make it do that, too.

Robin's book will show you the benefits of switching to Linux immediately. Your computer will run faster and more reliably than you ever believed possible. Surfing the net will no longer be an exercise in paranoia. And you'll discover a whole new world of powerful, free software that can run rings around the programs available for Windows.

It shouldn't matter what color your eggs are. After all, you're not eating the shells; you're eating what's inside. Nor should it matter what operating system you're using. The OS is just the foundation for the programs you really use to work and play. Truth is, many of you are already using Linux every day without knowing it. Tivo runs on Linux. So do many big web sites, including Amazon.com. The special effects for some of Hollywood's biggest movies were created on Linux, and Linux runs the billing for some of the world's largest companies.

Some day we won't know or care whether our digital devices use Windows, Linux, BSD, or OS X. We'll just know they work. But when that day comes, you'll be able to look back and say, we owe it all to Linus Torvalds, Richard Stallman, and the pioneers of the Free Software movement, who worked without pay to create the best free operating system ever, and to give us a choice when it seemed like everyone else was going bananas for Windows.

Leo Laporte
Petaluma, California (the former chicken and egg capital of the world)
August 24, 2004

Leo has been trying to get people to use Linux for years. He hosts *Call for Help* on G4TechTV Canada and can be heard every weekend on KFI 640 AM Los Angeles.

Introduction

We all want our computers to "just work." We want to view Web sites, exchange email, create letters and other printed material, do our book-keeping, and perform other basic computer tasks without worrying about viruses, spam, Web popup ads, system crashes or high program license fees.

Linux is the low-cost key to trouble-free computing. It's a little different from Windows or Mac, so you'll need to learn some new tricks to use it, but they are not hard tricks, and they won't take long to learn. In return for that little bit of learning, you'll be able to perform everyday computing tasks rapidly and easily without worrying about viruses, worms or spyware. In fact, after you have Linux installed and your favorite programs set up, you won't need to think about your computer at all. You'll be able to concentrate on what you're *doing* with it, whether you're creating a budget spreadsheet for your business, creating a family newsletter or downloading and listening to your favorite music.

This book and the instructional DVD video inside the front cover are based on MEPIS Linux. The *SimplyMEPIS* CD inside the back cover includes all the software you need to surf the Web, read and write email, do sophisticated word processing, make slide presentations, manipulate spreadsheets, upload and edit images from digital cameras and scanners, create Web sites, enjoy music or videos, play many hours' worth of entertaining games, and generally do what you and most other people expect a personal computer to do.

About the *Point & Click Linux!* DVD

It's not a single hour-long video, but a series of "bite-sized" short tutorials. Each one focuses on a specific function or program. The video tutorials contain most of the information in the printed book, but *show* you how to do things instead o *telling* you how to do them.

The DVD plays in standard NTSC (U.S. format) DVD players, and in computers equipped with DVD drives. Check this book's companion Web site, `PointAndClickLinux.com`, for added and updated videos.

Proprietary Windows software equivalent to the programs on your *SimplyMEPIS* CD, plus the current version of Windows itself, would cost at least $1500 or more. And if the included software doesn't cover all your needs, the MEPIS servers offer hundreds of other useful programs you can download right away and start using without paying another cent. Adventurous souls can experiment with any one of *thousands* of free non-MEPIS programs provided by the worldwide, volunteer-run Debian project with only a few mouse clicks—and can delete any programs that don't work out with another few clicks.

(Note that when you delete a MEPIS or Debian program, it is 100% gone. There is no "residue" or "registry crud" leftover as there often is in Windows when you try to delete a program you no longer want.)

While this book focuses on MEPIS, there is an appendix dedicated to other popular Linux distributions, because Linux is about choice, not about locking you into one way of doing things. You'll also be happy to know that the programs described in the following pages and on the included DVD video work the same way no matter which Linux distribution you choose. Even if you start with MEPIS and later move to another flavor of Linux, your learning time will not have been wasted.

But that's enough loose talk. Let's turn the page and get started with trouble-free, *Point & Click Linux!* computing.

Section I

Getting Started

1

Chapter 1

What You Can Do with Linux

Linux used to be hard to install and use. Now it's easy. The first version was written in 1991 as a hobby project by a computer science student, Linus Torvalds, who wanted a version of the industrial-strength Unix operating system that would run on his home computer. But Torvalds decided he'd learn more if, instead of trying to adapt commercial Unix to his computer, he wrote his own simple Unix-like operating system. So he did. Then he posted his creation on the Internet so others could not only use it freely, but also contribute improvements and additions to it. Several hundred programmers soon joined Torvalds' effort to create a new operating system, and within a few years their efforts resulted in a powerful operating system "kernel" that offered Unix-like stability and performance on inexpensive desktop hardware.

Early Linux was not intended for home or office computer users. It was a "raw guts" thing with screens that looked like this:

```
robin@0[robin]$ su
Password:
root@0[robin]# ifconfig
eth0      Link encap:Ethernet  HWaddr 00:02:E3:2E:C8:11
          inet addr:192.168.0.4  Bcast:192.168.0.255  Mask:255.255.255.0
          UP BROADCAST RUNNING MULTICAST  MTU:1500  Metric:1
          RX packets:1459931 errors:0 dropped:0 overruns:0 frame:0
          TX packets:3196776 errors:0 dropped:0 overruns:0 carrier:0
          collisions:0 txqueuelen:100
          RX bytes:1409990274 (1.3 GiB)  TX bytes:263244306 (251.0 MiB)
          Interrupt:3

lo        Link encap:Local Loopback
          inet addr:127.0.0.1  Mask:255.0.0.0
          UP LOOPBACK RUNNING  MTU:16436  Metric:1
          RX packets:2384182 errors:0 dropped:0 overruns:0 frame:0
          TX packets:2384182 errors:0 dropped:0 overruns:0 carrier:0
          collisions:0 txqueuelen:0
          RX bytes:175702915 (167.5 MiB)  TX bytes:175702915 (167.5 MiB)

root@0[robin]# 
```

We're obviously not talking "user friendly" here. During its first years of development, Linux was strictly intended for computer professionals, computer science students, and skilled hobbyists. But since then, thousands of programmers worldwide have worked to make Linux more useful for ordinary people like you and me. While it still has the computing power and stability of Unix, the face of Linux we now see is one we can use with simple point and click commands instead of typing long strings of text like

```
./configure —with-tls —enable-slurpd —enable-crypt —enable-syslog
-sysconfdir=/etc
```

That sort of thing is fine for professional systems administrators running groups of server computers, but those of us who use Linux on our PCs would rather see graphical buttons like these:

Obviously, if we click on a picture of a CD that has musical notes on it, we expect to play a music CD, and if we click on a picture of a printer, we expect to print something. This is how we control MEPIS Linux through its KDE desktop and KDE's underlying X Window graphics system, which translate our clicks into code our microprocessors understand. This happens in all operating systems, not just in Linux. Computers don't understand pictures and clicks, just binary code, and they don't "draw pictures" in the sense that we humans do, either. They turn colored dots on your computer screen on and off the same way your TV screen does. Beneath the pictures on all computer screens there is a whirring set of binary digits flying back and forth. Linux admits this is happening more than other operating systems do, and is also happy to tell you what it's doing in text format, which is what you see when you start your computer with the *SimplyMEPIS* CD and see text scrolling on the screen. Linux is methodically starting and testing each of your computer's many functions and is reporting its actions to you instead of hiding them. Most of the time you can ignore this text and treat it as something cool that looks like it came from a "Matrix" movie, but if your modem or hard drive ever stops working correctly, watching that "bootup" sequence can tell you what's wrong without a lot of tedious diagnostic work.

But most of the time we don't need to worry about how our computers work internally. The programmers who developed the GNU, X Window, and KDE components of our Linux system have already done all the worrying for us. We're here to use Linux for everyday computing tasks, not to become computer scientists.

When you boot your computer with the SimplyMEPIS CD in the back of this book, you will immediately be able to

1. View your favorite Web sites
2. Read and write email
3. Download music from the Internet
4. Read online documents published in Adobe Acrobat format
5. Write and print letters, memos, and other documents
6. Create and print spreadsheets in either numerical or graphical formats
7. Read and edit most documents created by Microsoft Office
8. Create eye-grabbing slide presentations
9. Do professional-level desktop publishing
10. Upload and edit images from digital cameras and most scanners
11. Draw pictures and save them in many graphics formats
12. Create Web pages and upload them to a server
13. Perform basic home and office bookkeeping tasks
14. Chat online with AIM, Yahoo Messenger, Microsoft Messenger or IRC

15. Play dozens of card, board, arcade, and educational games

You can do all this while running *SimplyMEPIS* from your CD drive, without installation. After you install *SimplyMEPIS* on your hard drive—which only takes a few clicks—you will be able to do much more. And when you learn the basics of running Linux—which won't take more than a few hours—you'll learn to customize the behavior and appearance of your Linux desktop and every program you use so they're the way *you* want them, not the

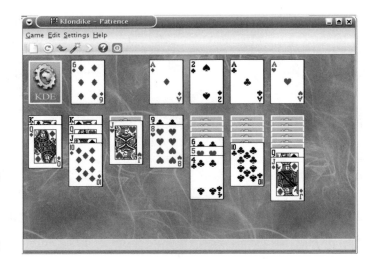

way some programmer decided they should be. This flexibility is one of the greatest features of Linux, one you'll learn to appreciate after a while even if you stick to default settings at first.

Another advantage you have with Linux is that you can easily install new programs without worrying about spyware, adware or viruses. You can get over 1,000 MEPIS-certified programs directly from the MEPIS servers in return for a small annual subscription fee (or have them shipped to you on CD for a small additional charge). You'll also get free support for all of them through the MEPIS online forums, even if you are not a paid subscriber. If you need specialized software that isn't on the MEPIS servers, or you choose not to subscribe, you can download any of over 10,000 free programs from the worldwide network of volunteer-maintained Debian Project servers. These programs aren't guaranteed to work with MEPIS, but 90% of them will work just fine. It's just as simple to uninstall a program in Linux as it is to install it, so if you try one and it doesn't work out, it's no big deal.

Running Windows Programs in Linux

There are commercial programs you can buy that allow you to run Windows programs you already own. Although you are probably better off in the long run if you make use of "native" Linux programs for as many tasks as possible, you may have a few Windows pro-

grams you aren't quite ready to give up. Toward the end of this book you'll find instructions on how to get and install CodeWeavers' CrossOver Office and CrossOver Plugin packages that allow many Windows programs to work in Linux without having a copy of Windows on your computer at all. You'll also find information about Win4Lin, a program that lets you run a copy of Windows 95, 98 or ME (and virtually any Windows program) *inside* Linux. This is different from "dual-booting" Windows and Linux on the same computer for several reasons:

"Dual-booting" means you have both Windows and Linux installed on your computer, which is easy to do with MEPIS, but to change from one operating system to the other you must reboot your computer.

Windows typically starts and runs faster through Win4Lin in Linux than it does all by itself. This sounds strange, but it's true.

If Windows crashes while you're using it through Win4Lin, the whole computer doesn't need to be restarted, just Windows itself, and this takes a lot less time than going through the whole boot-from-scratch rigmarole.

While using Windows under Linux through Win4Lin, you can use the Konqueror file manager included with MEPIS to drop a picture you've created with your Windows software directly into a Web page or other document you're creating with a Linux program. This versatility lets you use the best Windows programs and the best Linux programs side by side, so you have the best of both worlds at your fingertips, instead of having to choose one or the other.

In the end, even if you decide you still want to use some Windows programs for a while, you'll probably find that many Linux programs aren't "just as good" or "almost as good" as the Windows programs you're used to using—they are better than their Windows equivalents in many ways and include useful features they lack.

The (free) Mozilla Messenger email program we've included for you is totally immune to all viruses and worms that can infect Microsoft Outlook or Outlook Express, and it has (free) built-in spam filtering that is better than most of the filters you can buy as add-ons for Microsoft's email programs.

The Mozilla browser in *SimplyMEPIS* has many features Explorer lacks. It can easily block annoying "popup" Web ads, and it has a "tabbed browsing" feature that makes it easy to open many pages at once from your favorite news site—or from a catalog site while you're shopping online—then close all those pages with a single click.

OpenOffice.org (OOo), the strangely named office package we've included, can save documents in many formats Microsoft Office can't, including Adobe's PDF, so you can publish the same creation on the Internet, on paper, and on a CD without having to rewrite it for each medium. It's also more versatile than Microsoft Office in another way: It can read, edit, and save documents in PDF and Microsoft Office formats, but Microsoft Office can't read or edit documents created in the native OOo format or create PDF files. Another advantage you'll have with OOo is that it automatically "compresses" each document you save so it takes up much less of your hard drive than documents saved by Microsoft Office. OOo will seem strange at first, if you're used to Microsoft Office, but with a little practice you'll find that, beyond its file format versatility, it has many features Microsoft Office doesn't that can make your work faster and easier.

The K3B CD/DVD creation software we've chosen for MEPIS is the best full-featured "burner" program we've ever used, in any operating system. You drag the files you want on your CD or DVD into the K3B window, press "burn," and you're done. It automatically detects and sets up almost all common CD and DVD "write" drives, too, and doesn't require special "drivers" for any of them.

These are just a few examples. You'll find many other programs worth your love as you explore Linux, including specialized software for scientific research, video and audio editing, web hosting, and software development. We all have different software needs, and no one book—or one CD—can cover them all.

In this book and the accompanying video DVD and software CD, we concentrate on software for everyday home and office desktop computing so you can start using Linux right away for everyday tasks. After you get comfortable with Linux on your desktop, you can start exploring its power in other areas, all the way up to building your own world-class supercomputer by linking hundreds or even thousands of Linux PCs together.

But we'll worry about building a Linux supercomputer next week (or maybe next year). Right now, let's put that *SimplyMEPIS* CD in your computer's CD drive and spend an hour or two mastering Linux basics.

Chapter 2

Running the
SimplyMEPIS CD

MEPIS runs as a "Live CD" without installation. On most PCs, running MEPIS Linux is as simple as putting the *SimplyMEPIS* CD in your CD drive and restarting your computer. After a little bit of whirring, you'll see a list of menu choices.

While this menu gives you a number of choices, in most cases you can just wait a few seconds and let the default selection run automatically. If the default selection does not start correctly—that is, if you see nothing but a blank screen—you will need to experiment with the available choices until you find the one that best suits your computer. (Pay particular attention to the "Monitor Resolution" choice. Each make of monitor has a maximum resolution and will not display beyond it.) We also advise trying several different kernel choices. The Linux kernel is the "heart"' of your operating system, and some versions work noticeably faster than others on some computers. It only takes a few seconds to try each kernel selection. You don't need to go through a long shutdown procedure for each test; just shut your computer off with the power button, turn it back on, and when the menu comes up, make a different menu choice each time.

Another pitfall you may encounter is a total refusal by your computer to read the CD, in which case you will not see the menu screen shown above until you change your computer's BIOS settings.

Making Your Computer Boot from a CD

If your computer starts from the CD and runs *SimplyMEPIS* the first time you try, you don't need to read this section.

But some users have computers that refuse to boot from their CD drives instead of their hard drives. This is not a Linux thing. Many PCs come from the factory with their BIOS (the Basic Input/Output System that comes with the motherboard) set to boot only from the hard drive. Changing the boot order is not hard—when you know how to do it—and if you don't already know how to do this, it's a great trick to master not only for Linux use but also if you ever need to install a new version of Windows or reinstall your old one as part of normal maintenance.

Not all computers use the same commands to get you into the BIOS setup (or just "Setup" as some call it on their boot screens). If you're lucky, when your computer first starts it will tell you what to do as it boots up, with a little note like "Setup: F1" that probably scrolls by before you can hit the F1 key. No problem; shut the computer off with the switch (you don't need to use the operating system shutdown procedure because the operating system hasn't started yet), and have your finger ready this time. But before you begin messing with your BIOS, please read this bold-face note:

> **WARNING:**
>
> Be very, very careful when you change anything in your BIOS. Make exact notes of the original settings before you change anything at all, and read all the little "how to change/how to save" text at the bottom of the screen very carefully. If you mess up your BIOS your computer may not boot any OS, and if you set something you shouldn't and it still boots, vital functions may not work correctly. Be very, very careful when you change anything in your BIOS.

That said, when you get into your BIOS setup you'll probably see a screen that has words like "BOOT PRIORITY" or "BOOT ORDER" somewhere on it. This is what you need to change. (Your mouse may not work at this point. If it doesn't, you will need to use your Tab or up and down arrow keys to move between lines.)

When you get your cursor on the "BOOT" line, you can usually change the boot priority by hitting the space bar. If this doesn't work, try other keys. You can't hurt anything at this point. It's only when you save changes that you can damage your system, and every common BIOS has an option for "Exit without saving changes" you can use if you're not absolutely, positively sure you did the right thing.

Obviously, you want "CD-ROM" to be the first boot choice if you're going to be booting from a CD-ROM. After you do your new installation (or need to return temporarily to the operating system you already have installed) you can change the boot priority back to the way it was before your experiment.

Think of BIOS Access as a Puzzle to Be Figured Out

One HP desktop we use for a test computer doesn't just give you a single BIOS screen. First, you hit F10 to access the BIOS setup program, then you choose "Advanced CMOS Setup" from a menu to find your boot priority. The instructions are all there, right on the screen, but you need to read them instead of just clicking keys and hoping.

11

Other manufacturers have other little BIOS tricks. After you've become accustomed to changing BIOS settings you won't have trouble figuring them out. Only the first few times are hard. If you think carefully before you *save*, and make sure you read all the text on the BIOS setup screens before you start making changes (and take notes before you start hitting keys, so that you can return to the default settings easily), you'll figure it all out without fuss.

A List of Common BIOS Access Commands

We compiled this list from various online sources. It is not complete, but covers some of the most common computer manufacturers' most popular products. If your computer isn't listed, try some of the most common access commands; you can't hurt anything by trying them. And if that fails, your computer or motherboard manufacturer's documentation or Web site is a sure source of information about your BIOS, and is the ultimate place to turn. You'll need to know your computer's exact model number (and possibly serial number) to get the right commands, because they vary from motherboard to motherboard, and computer manufacturers can (and often do) change motherboard suppliers in the middle of a production run without telling anyone.

1. Acer—F1, F2, CTRL+ALT+ESC
2. AST—CTRL+ALT+ESC, CTRL+ALT+DEL
3. Compaq—F1 or F10
4. Dell—400 F1 or F3
5. Dell—Dimension F2 or DEL
6. Dell—Inspiron F2
7. Dell—Latitude F2
8. Dell—Optiplex DEL or F2
9. Dell—Precision F2
10. eMachine—DEL
11. Gateway—F1 or F2
12. HP—F1, F2 or F10

13. IBM (PC) —F1

14. IBM E-pro Laptop—F2

15. IBM PS/2—CTRL+ALT+INS after CTRL+ALT+DEL

16. Micron—F1, F2 or DEL

17. Sony®—VIAO F2 or F3

18. Tiger—DEL

19. Toshiba—ESC or F1

If You Can't Figure Out How to Change Your BIOS Settings…

…make a boot floppy. Here's how you do it in Windows:

1. Start Windows.
2. Place the *SimplyMEPIS* CD in your CD drive with Windows running.
3. Open a DOS Window (in Windows).
4. Go to the linux directory on the CD.
5. Insert a blank, formatted floppy disk in your floppy drive.
6. Execute mkbootfloppy.bat.
7. Reboot with the floppy in your floppy drive and the *SimplyMEPIS* CD in your CD drive. Your computer should now run *SimplyMEPIS*.

Booting MEPIS

Linux is very methodical in the way it starts. Each function of your computer is tested. This means your Linux startup may be slower than in other operating systems, but sometimes "slow but sure" is best. Another thing that's slowing things down is that you're running your software from the CD drive instead of from the hard drive. CD drives are much slower than hard drives, to the point where anything you do from the LiveCD is going to seem like it's happening in slow motion instead of at full speed. You'll find that after you get MEPIS installed on your hard drive, everything will take place between two and ten times as fast as it does when you're running from the CD.

Why MEPIS Linux Asks for a Password

After the startup routine, the screen may either look funny, like static, or go blank for a second. Then you'll see a login screen that gives you two choices: "Demo" and "root."

It's best to start with the user name *demo* rather than use *root,* especially if you intend to connect to the Internet. This is a security measure, and is one of the big reasons Linux doesn't fall prey to the viruses and worms that plague the users of some other operating systems. When you are logged in as a *user*—probably your own name once you get MEPIS Linux installed permanently—the only part of the system you will be able to change is your own data and things like screen color and some other appearance options. To install software or make any heavy changes to the system, Linux requires you to log in as *root*. If you are logged in as a *user*, malicious hackers can't easily install software you don't know about or perform other mischief.

Cats, children and well-meaning friends can't mess up your computer by typing in the wrong commands, either, as long as you are logged in as a *user* and not as *root*. In fact, when you do the actual Linux installation you'll be able to give other users their own user accounts so they can log in and use your computer without disturbing (or ever seeing) your private information, email or anything else you store in your computer. And each user can choose his or her screen colors and other custom features, too, including Web site bookmarks and favorite music. With Linux, a whole family can share a computer, but it can be a "personal computer" for each family member since each can have his or her own user login.

Only root gets to see everything. (That's going to be you, right?)

Logging In

In "demo mode," the password for the demo user is *demo*, all lowercase. The root password is *root*, also lowercase. We'll show you how to change passwords (and add users) later, when we install MEPIS on your hard drive. But right now, let's go with these defaults. Enter them, click on the "login" button—or just hit your "Enter" key after you type in the password—and in a second or two you'll see your full, ready-to-use KDE desktop. If your PC has speakers, you should hear a few notes of music as the desktop appears.

If everything has gone right, you are now ready to work (or play) with Linux. If your

computer is connected to the Internet through a network cable attached to a DSL line, cable modem or other high-speed "always on" setup, you should be connected to the Internet now. You can test this by clicking the "M" in the panel at the bottom of the screen, which starts the Mozilla Web browser that's included in *SimplyMEPIS*.

If your network is not operating correctly at this point—that is, if you're not able to view Web sites—you need to open the MEPIS system center and change your system settings. If you're online automatically, there is no need to do this, but it still might be nice to spend a minute looking at the System Center.

Using the MEPIS System Center

To open the MEPIS System Center, click on the "S" icon on the main desktop.

The first thing you get when you open the MEPIS System Center is a login screen. This one asks for the *root* password, not your *user* password. While you're running from the CD, the password is *root*. (You'll change it to something more secure after you install MEPIS on your hard drive, of course.)

The Magic Desktop-Clearing Icon

We just told you to click on an icon on the desktop. What if your screen is covered by an application window? Or two or three or 40 application windows? (Linux has no practical limit on the number of applications or windows you can keep open, so you really *can* have 40—or even 100—applications open at the same time.)

The answer is the *View Desktop* icon in the lower left hand corner of your screen, next to the small picture of the gear with a "K" on top of it. Click the *View Desktop* icon, and you'll have a clear view of your blank desktop.

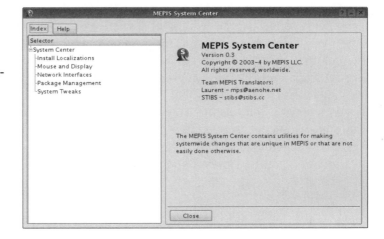

Type in that password, and you'll see the MEPIS System Center main screen.

On the left side of this screen, you see an index of functions, and above that index there's a *Help* choice. If you click *Help*, you'll see these words:

Using the MEPIS System Center

To use the MEPIS System Center, just select a function in the Index tab and follow the instructions in this Help tab.

That's how simple it is to use the MEPIS System Center. We'll start by looking at *Network Interface*.

This screen tells us what our network is doing. In this example, we have an active wireless network connection. We see which network services are running because we have buttons available that allow us to stop them. If those services aren't run-

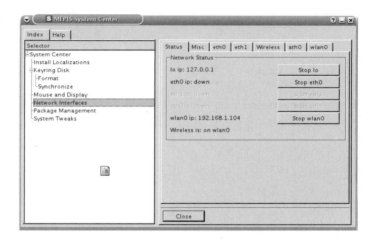

ning, those buttons say "Start" instead of "Stop." The buttons marked "Start eth0" and "Start ath0" are shadowed and barely visible because this computer was not attached to a wired (eth0) connection, just wireless, so no wired connection was detected.

Ath0 is used only for *Atheros* network cards, which aren't terribly common. If you have one, MEPIS automatically detects it, automatically installs the right drivers, and automatically starts it for you.

Look Ma, No Drivers!

With Windows and other operating systems, you often need to install a specific software "driver" for network cards from CDs supplied by the cards' manufacturers. MEPIS Linux has drivers for almost all the popular network cards, including wireless cards, built in. It also has built-in drivers for most popular digital cameras, scanners, printers, and other devices you're likely to attach to your computer. (If you want to add hardware that was made after this book was written, you may need to get an updated version of MEPIS that includes drivers for it, but that's not hard. We'll show you how to do that in Chapter 24, "Downloading and Installing Software.")

As a rule, MEPIS will run any common wire-connected network card without you doing anything. Wireless may or may not start on its own, but it's easy to make sure "wlan0" is running and start it if it's not. Click on the "Wireless" tab, click the "Use auto-config" choice and click "Apply" if starting "wlan0" didn't make your wireless connection come to life.

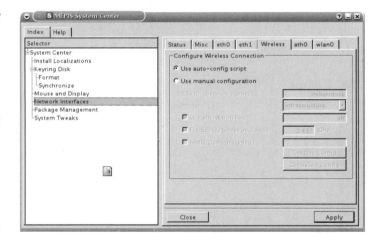

If you're using a wireless network with encryption and other non-default settings, you'll want to click "Use Manual Configuration" and set MEPIS to conform to your network's setup, which you can determine by accessing your wireless hub's setup utility and instructions.

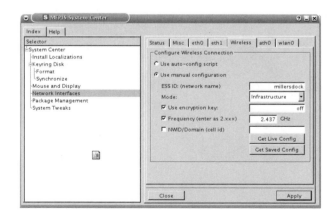

Even if all the setup instructions that came with your wireless hub were written for Windows, the numbers and settings are identical for all operating systems. Type them in the appropriate blanks, click "Apply," and they should work without any problem.

Dialup and PPPoE Connections

Dialup modem users should turn to Chapter 5, "KPPP—Easy Modem Dialer Application." We put it there because KPPP is only one of several dialup connection programs available for Linux. While KPPP is our favorite, you may later decide to download and use one of the others.

DSL users whose providers still use PPPoE (Point-to-Point Protocol over Ethernet) directly may need to use the KDSL utility to connect, but should first make sure their providers don't have newer router-style modems available that will eliminate the need for a login and password. Virtually all major U.S. DSL providers have switched to router-style modems, which are detected and set up automatically by MEPIS Linux. (These DSL modems are far more efficient than the old PPPoE ones were, anyway, so you should make this switch no matter what operating system you use.)

Printer Setup

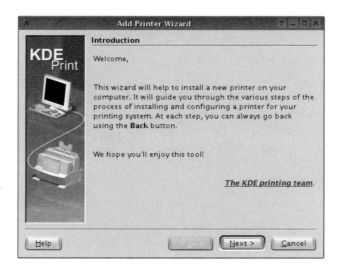

MEPIS Linux includes drivers for popular home and small office printers. To set up your printer, click the "K-Gear" icon on your panel, select "Print System" and choose "Add Printer." This brings up the "Add Printer Wizard."

If you have your Internet connection figured out now and you want to read about the development and capabilities of the KDE printing system, click on the underlined words "The KDE printing team" and the `http://printing.kde.org` Web site will open. But this is not really necessary. What we really need to do now is click "Next."

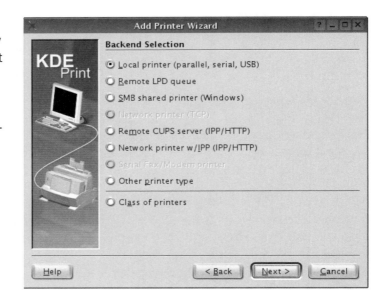

For this basic tutorial, we're assuming you have a printer directly connected to your computer through parallel, serial or USB port, so we'll select "Local printer," then click "Next."

(For more information on how to use a printer connected to another computer on your network, click the "Help" button to bring up a copy of *The KDE Print Handbook* or go to the `printing.kde.org` Web site, which may have a newer version.)

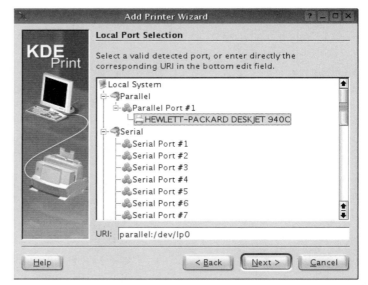

Now it's time to select how your printer is connected to your computer and click on that choice. (Scroll down for USB and some other choices.) Again, click "Next" when you're done.

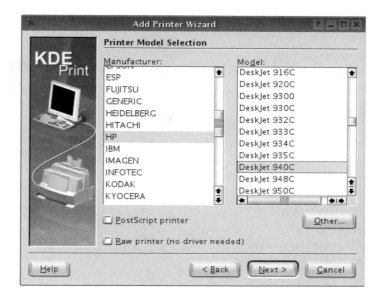

Pick your printer make and model from the lists. If your exact printer model isn't listed (which is unlikely), choose one from the same manufacturer with a similar model number.

For this demonstration, we're using a common HP Deskjet 940C. Naturally, you're using *your* printer, not the one *we* happen to have handy. And, of course, click "Next."

Some printers have more than one driver available. To learn more about one of the drivers, click on it, then click "Driver Information" and a page about that driver will pop up. So far we've never gone wrong choosing the recommended driver, so we're going to stick with that one. And click "Next."

Now we print a test page to make sure that everything's working right. (If you're asked to enter your root password, remember that

while you're running MEPIS from CD, it's *root*.) While writing this chapter and taking screenshots for it, we had one problem: The test page wouldn't print because the printer wasn't plugged into the computer. MEPIS Linux is forgiving and user-friendly, but there are limits to what it can do, and an unplugged printer is beyond its control. After we plugged the printer in, everything worked fine.

An important note about printer operation: Your printer may not work correctly with most programs while running from the LiveCD instead of from Linux installed on your hard drive. When you are running Linux through your CD drive, the print program is not stored on your hard drive where the programs you use (like word processors) look for it when you tell them you want to print. As long as the test page prints, you're fine even if other pages don't. After you actually install MEPIS Linux, you'll have no trouble printing.

Shutting Down

This is the last function we need to master. Hard? Not exactly. Here's how you do it:

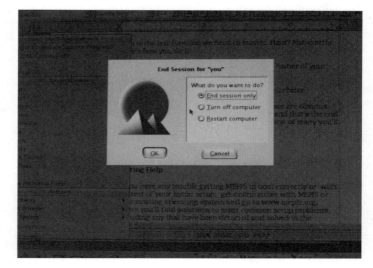

1. Click on the K-Gear logo at the lower left corner of your screen.
2. Click on "Logout"— the bottom menu choice.

You have three choices. Their purposes are obvious. Pick the one you prefer, and click it. That's the end of this Linux session, hopefully the first of many you'll run in coming years.

Getting Help

If you have any trouble getting MEPIS to boot correctly or with the rest of your initial setup, get online either with MEPIS or your existing operating system and go to www.mepis.org. You'll find solutions to most common setup problems, including any that have been detected and solved in the months between the day this book was written and the day you first picked it up.

And if you don't see an answer on the MEPIS site itself, go to www.mepis.org/forum, where MEPIS developers and experienced users can give you one-on-one help. (There is no charge to use the MEPIS forums.)

Chapter 3

Working with Linux: KDE and KWrite

Now that we have MEPIS running, let's play with it a little. We'll explore some basic Linux functions here, including how to make, save, find, and move files, using a simple bit of text as an example. This is also the point where video instructions start coming into their own. Sometimes it's easier to see how to do things when someone demonstrates how they work and talks you through the process instead of just giving you descriptions on a printed page.

The KDE desktop is the "public face" of MEPIS Linux. Remember, no matter what operating system we use, the microprocessor at the heart of our computer deals with information strictly in the form of binary "either it's on or it's off" digits. All operating systems have several layers of software designed to hide those binary operations from you and put a pretty face on them. In Linux, the most common interface between the computer's guts and what you see on the screen is called the X Window system. The KDE Desktop, which works with the X Window system, is the GUI (Graphical User Interface) that makes Linux look nice to human eyes and gives us the ability to "Point and Click" commands instead of typing them in. There are other Linux GUIs, notably the well-regarded Gnome desktop, that you can try later, but we decided to start with KDE because it's the most popular and generally considered the easiest one to learn for new Linux users.

KDE is almost infinitely customizable—you can choose any desktop background you like, and move almost everything on that desktop to wherever you want it, as we'll show in a later chapter—but right now we are going to talk about how to use the KDE desktop in the default configuration it loaded from your *SimplyMEPIS* CD.

The first thing that strikes your eye is that there are several small, captioned  pictures or "Icons" along the left side of your screen, and a bunch more along the bottom in the "panel" we use to control most functions in MEPIS Linux. To do almost anything with your computer, you start by clicking on one of these icons. If you want to play a tune from a CD, you click on the CD picture. A window will pop up that shows what's on the music CD you (hopefully) put in your CD drive before trying this. (If there's no CD, you'll get a notice that there's no media in the CD drive.)

"Mount Partitions" shows all the storage devices attached to your computer, including your hard drive. In this example, you see several hard drive partitions. (We'll explain hard drive partitioning in the next chapter.) You'll also see cdrom, floppy, and sda1. "Floppy" is a floppy disk drive, "sda1" is a Flash card reader con-

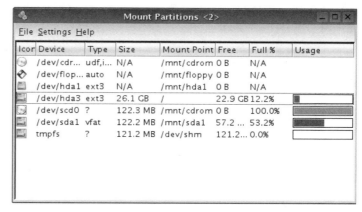

taining photos from a digital camera, and "cdrom" is the CD drive. If you don't have a USB storage device or floppy drive, you won't see those options; but either way, it's obvious that to check the contents of the CD, you click on the CD picture.

Now you get another "menu" that shows all the files on the CD. In this case, it's music. Pick which tune you want to listen to, click on it, and it plays. That's the way things work with KDE. You point at an icon, click on it, and you get what you want.

> Note: You can open a CD in your CD drive either with the CD icon or through the *Mount Partitions* menu. Linux and KDE often give you more than one way to do things. Always feel free to choose the one that's most comfortable for you.

The KDE Panel

The bar across the bottom of your screen is the "Panel," as in "Control

Panel," and it's an important part of our desktop. The "K-Gear" icon at the left end accesses the logout and shutdown menus and, literally, the menus that take you to all programs on your computer. The icon next to the "K-Gear" that looks like a pen writing on a desktop is for the "View Desktop" utility that hides all program windows currently open so you that can see the icons on the main desktop. The icons to its right open specific programs.

(The icons currently visible here are for programs this book's author and the MEPIS developers believe most people are most likely to use. Later, we'll show you how to delete their selections and add your own if you like. It's easy to do.)

To the right of the program icons you have your "Taskbar." This shows what programs you currently have open. As you gain experience with Linux you'll start to realize that you can open many programs at the same time instead of sticking to one or two. With a crowded desktop, the only way to keep track of your opened programs is the taskbar, and clicking on programs' entries in the taskbar is the easiest way to switch from one to another.

To the taskbar's right are several cool little utilities, including sound control. Go ahead and click on them. See what they do.

Konqueror— the KDE File Manager

The window we saw when we clicked on the CD icon in the window that opened wasn't from a special CD-playing program, but part of the Konqueror file manager, which we use to find, save, and move files of all kinds. In Linux (and KDE) every-thing is a file. You can have picture files, music files, text files, program files, even nail files—or at least files you name "nail" if you are writing a series of research papers about carpentry through the ages, or you're a cosmetologist who takes pictures of extra-cute fingernail decorations you've done.

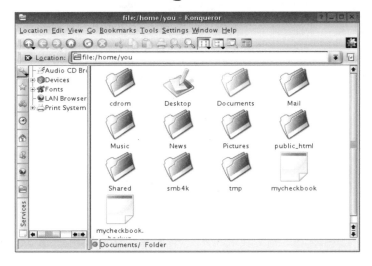

You are the boss of your file system. In *SimplyMEPIS*, we already set up some basic folders where you can save documents, pictures, and other common kinds of information. You can easily add your own folders with names like "Baby Pictures" or "Tropical Drink Recipes," and even have them appear on the desktop so you can easily find them later.

If you want to add a folder called "Sunsets" and want it to show on your desktop, click on "Desktop," where you'll see the icons that are already on your desktop. With your cursor (the little pointer your mouse or other pointer-moving device moves around your screen) anywhere in the

blank space in this window, click your right mouse button. You'll see a little list of things you can do, and the top item is "Create new," with an arrow to the right of the words. Slide your cursor to the right, over that arrow, and you'll see several choices. The top one is "Folder," and that's the one we want. Click on it with your left button.

You have just popped up what we call a "dialog box" that asks you to type in some sort of needed information. It says, "Enter folder name:" and right below those words there is a little space—a "form"—with the words "New Folder" in it. Your cursor is already in that little form, and unless you want your new folder to be named "New Folder" you want to hit your "backspace" or "delete" key (either will work), then type in our chosen name, "Sunsets."

Click "OK" and your new "Sunsets" folder will now show up on your desktop. It's going to be a great place to store some of your favorite beach sunset photos. (And suddenly that "Tropical Drink Recipes" folder sounds like a good idea, too, doesn't it?)

How Your System's "File Tree" Works

Files are stored in an "inverted tree" structure, with the roots at the top and the branches growing downward. In fact, the master directory for your Linux system is called "root" and is represented by a / (that's the "forward slash" under the question mark on your keyboard.) Moving down, you see a list of main folders, called "directories." You can see what's in any of them any time you like by clicking

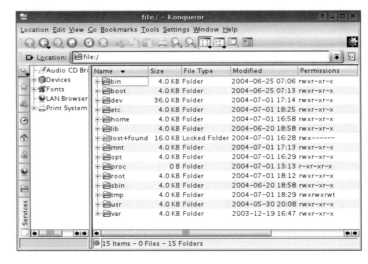

the little "+" and opening up that branch of the "tree," but the only directory we need to think about 99% of the time is /home, because that's where our personal files live.

To go directly to your Home directory from your desktop, click the "Home" icon—the one that looks like a little house—at the bottom of your screen.

You see folders there. Click on one of the folders and you move out onto one of the branches of the directory tree. We already created one folder of our own, and we can create all we want, folders within folders within folders until our minds spin. However, it's usually easier to keep everything simple so we can remember where we filed things and access them with the fewest possible number of clicks through folders and sub-folders.

There are several ways you can view your file system. Most people seem to prefer icons, with pictures and text files set so you see a little "preview" of them as the icon. This is the default style. In our "Beyond the Basics" section we'll show you how to use several others.

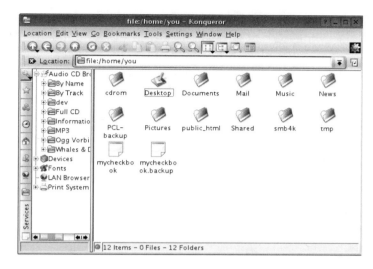

How you arrange your Home directory's file system is up to you. We gave you a basic "starter" set of folders to get you going, and to keep things simple we'll only deal with them right now. After you've mastered a few more Linux basics—by the end of this book—you'll be ready to customize your file system, along with almost everything else, to suit your taste rather than ours.

Your First Application—KWrite

We're going to stop talking about the KDE desktop and file manager for a moment and focus on the simple text editor, KWrite, that's built into KDE. This will give us a chance to create, save, move and copy an actual text file. Because KWrite is a KDE program, it looks and acts just like all other KDE programs (and like most Linux programs in general, whether or not they're part of KDE). Therefore, what we

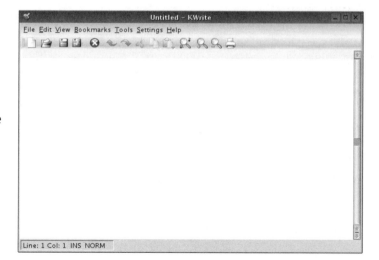

learn in the next few minutes will help us use all the software included on your *SimplyMEPIS* CD, along with any software you add to your system later.

To open KWrite, click on the bottom-of-the-screen icon that looks like a little notepad with a pencil sticking out of it. KWrite is exactly what that icon implies—a simple program for taking notes or writing basic text messages. It doesn't allow you to add italic or boldface or make type bigger or smaller in different lines. It is about as close as you can come, on a computer, to typing on a piece of paper with an old-fashioned typewriter or taking notes with a pad and pencil.

To start making a file in KWrite, type something. That's it. No setup is required.

Type in a paragraph or two.

Now let's demonstrate a very basic Linux trick: "One click" text copying. Highlight a few of the words you have just typed by placing the cursor in front of the first word you want to copy, hold down the left mouse button, and move your cursor over the words you want to copy while you keep holding that button. When you have

highlighted your chosen words, let go of the mouse button and, without touching it, move your cursor to the end of the last line you typed, then click both buttons at the same time (or the center button or scroll wheel if you have a three-button or scrollwheel mouse).

After a little practice, you'll find that this is a much faster way to paste text than pressing control keys., If you're totally in the habit of

Windows-style copying, where you press "Ctrl+C" to save highlighted text and "Ctrl+V" to paste it, you can still do it that way if you like.

You have several ways to delete text. Highlight what you want to delete, click on the scissors above, and it's gone. Or press the "Delete" key and it's gone. Or backspace from where you are back to where you want to stop deleting. Or place your cursor at a point where you want to delete everything *after* that point and hit "Delete." All three methods work.

To undelete, you go to the top of the KWrite window, click on "Edit," and click "Undo"—which is handily the top choice. If you want to save half a second, hold the "Ctrl" key while you press the letter "Z." This does the same thing.

Keyboard Shortcuts

Most Linux programs have lots of keyboard shortcuts you can use to replace the menu pointing. We'll cover many of them, but leave you to discover some of the less-common ones for yourself.

Anyway, we have now created text, copied it, and deleted a few words—then undeleted them. These are the basic things we do with a basic text editor. We have two main functions left to explore: "Print" and "Save."

Printing is dirt-simple: Click on the little picture of the printer in the top of the window, at the right side of the line of icons we call the "toolbar." If you have your printer set up the way we showed you earlier, your text will print. It won't have any fancy formatting but will look just like a typewritten page, because that's all a basic text editor is supposed to do.

"Save" takes a bit more work, but not a lot. The big questions are, "Where do you want to save your note?" and, "What name will you give it?"

This is where we apply what we learned about the file system. If this note is a draft you might want to work on later, perhaps you'll want to save it on your Desktop so it'll catch your eye later. If it's a "Tropical Drink Recipe" (and you made that folder), that's obviously where it belongs, and the title should be the name of the drink, like "Purple Mimosa."

The two main rules about saving files:

1. Save them in a pattern that makes sense to *you*—and maintain that pattern so you don't need to fumble around looking for them.
2. Use file names that make sense to *you* so you remember what was in them when you see them three months later.

(Note the *you* in there. It's *your* personal computer. Unless you're using it at work, and your company tells you how to file different types of information, you choose the way *you* like best, not the way someone else likes it.)

To save your document the first time, click either the little floppy disk picture in the toolbar or the floppy disk picture next to it that has a pencil on it. Either way will bring up a dialog box that asks you where you want to save your work and what you want to call it.

Because this is a "document" you may want to put it in your "Home" top-level folder or in a folder you have created. Or perhaps you will choose to put it on your Desktop. Either way, click on the appropriate folder, then type your name for this folder in the form called "Location" (which has that name because you're deciding the "file location" where this piece of work will be stored). Then click "Save" and you're saved.

After you've saved this little bit of text once, to save subsequent modifications you make to it, just click the floppy disk icon and the update will save automatically—or type "Ctrl+S" (shorthand for "Hold down the "Ctrl" key and press the "S" key) and you'll get the same results. You can also click on the "Edit" choice in the program's top menu, and you'll see "Save" and "Save As" choices there.

The only reason to use "Save As" on a piece of work you have already saved is if you want to resave it under a different title (location) or in a different format. We'll talk more about saving in different formats when we start talking about full-fledged word processing with OpenOffice.org and items we create with other programs more complicated than KWrite, which only saves your work as raw text. Yes, if you poke around in the menus you'll see an "Export" choice that leads to "HTML." But all you get when you do that is the HTML "pre" command that makes your text look, on the Web, just as if it came from a typewriter, not "real" HTML, which we can (and will) create with other programs later.

Configuring KWrite

Although KWrite obviously works without any configuration, this is a good time to spend a minute configuring Linux software. In our "Beyond the Basics" section we'll show you how to customize your software and, indeed, your entire desktop. This is just a taste here, and because we're running from a CD instead of from a hard drive, any changes we make now will be lost when we turn our computer off, so there's no way you can harm anything by experimenting.

We configure KWrite (and other KDE programs) by clicking on "Settings," then choosing "Configure Editor" from the list of choices.

This brings up a window that gives us choices.

It's easier and faster for you to experiment with those choices than to describe them, so we'll leave you to

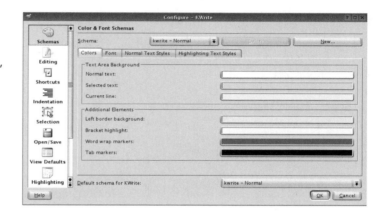

play with them on your own, but don't feel you're being abandoned without anyone to hold your hand while you experiment. In the lower left corner of that configuration screen you'll see a "Help" button. Click on it, and you'll see a complete manual for KWrite.

Another way to access that manual from the main program is to click on the "Help" menu item at the top of your KWrite window. Almost every KDE program—indeed, almost every Linux program—has a similar manual built-in, accessed through a "Help" button. Some of these built-in "Help" files are great, and some of them are not. (KWrite's Help happens to be one of the good ones.)

Most "Help" files have a way to contact the program's developers directly with bug reports, and those bug reports are invariably read and almost always acted upon. Bugs in KDE are usually fixed far faster than commercial software companies fix *their* bugs. (This is part of the "Magic of Open Source" we'll talk about at the end of the book, after we get you up to speed using Linux, which is our primary goal right now.)

This is enough about KWrite. We'll work with more commands—and extend our knowledge of Linux as we learn how to use other programs—after we get MEPIS Linux installed on our hard drive.

Chapter 4

Installing MEPIS Linux on Your Hard Drive

MEPIS

The great thing about a "Live CD" operating system like MEPIS Linux is that we've gotten a little experience with it before taking the step of actually installing it. We know where to get help and answers to questions (www.mepis.org and www.mepis.org/forum), and we have an idea of what software will be installed along with the basic operating system.

Note that we're not just installing an operating system, but all the software we need to perform basic computing tasks, plus enough games to divert us when we get bored with work—and we're also installing utilities like a junk email filter, popup blocker, and a firewall so that our computer is safe and secure when we connect to the Internet.

Now comes the big decision: If we already have Windows on our computer, do we want to keep it there, next to our new Linux installation? It is far easier to do a pure Linux install than to set up our computer as a "dual boot" machine, but let's grit our teeth and start by learning how to install MEPIS Linux while leaving Windows on our system.

> Note: This only works if you have at least a 10GB hard drive. If you have a lot of pictures, music, and other files that take up large amounts of hard drive space, you probably shouldn't try to have both Windows and Linux on your hard drive unless it can hold 20GB or more. At this point, if you have doubts about your hard drive's capacity, you may want to consider a total conversion to Linux instead of going the dual-boot route. (Failing that, you may consider adding a second hard drive to your computer or replacing your current hard drive with a bigger one.)

Setting Up a Dual-boot Linux/Windows System

You can skip these next few pages if you're ready to work with Linux full-time. But if you are going to keep Windows on your computer along with Linux, you must follow the following instructions *very carefully* or you may end up unable to run either operating system without reinstalling one or the other.

The first two things you must do have to do with Windows, not Linux:

1. Back up any critical data.
2. Defragment your hard drive. (This is a Windows utility; Windows manuals will tell you how to do this.)

Now it's time to embark on the adventure of hard drive repartitioning. To do this, open the MEPIS Installation Center by clicking on the appropriate desktop icon.

You'll need to put the root password here. Remember, while we're still running from CD, it's *root*, but we're going to choose a more secure one during our installation.

About hard drive partitions

Hard drives store data in the usual digital "on or off" style, but there are a number of different patterns in which they can be stored. Windows 95, 98, and ME use a method called FAT 32. Windows NT, 2000 and XP use a method called NTFS. DOS and really old versions of Windows use FAT 16. Linux uses a different method of data storage, and even uses different names for different drives. Windows usually calls floppy drives *A* and *B*, hard drive *C*, and CD drives *D*, unless there are two or more hard drives, in which case hard drives can be *E* and *F* and *G* and so on, with the CD drive becoming the letter after the last hard drive.

This illustration shows how Linux names drives:

/dev/flop is a floppy, */dev/cdr* is a CD drive, and */dev/hda* is this computer's single hard drive. There's also a *tempfs* that's a temporary file system designed to speed up certain kinds of data access, originally developed for huge mainframe computers but also useful

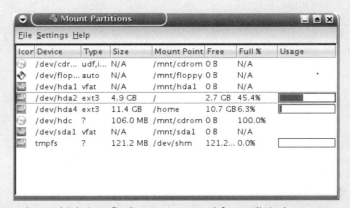

on your PC. There's also */dev/sda1*, which is a flash memory card for a digital camera.

Continues

Now comes the cool partition stuff.

While Windows typically uses the whole hard drive as one big glop, you can make Windows run slightly faster by partitioning the hard drive so it acts like a number of small hard drives instead of one big one. This can also make system maintenance easier. If you keep all your pictures and text files in a separate partition from your programs, you can back up all your important data by simply backing up that partition.

MEPIS Linux uses three partitions—what you see in the previous illustration as *hda2* and *hda4*, and another, very small *hda3* "swap" partition (that acts like an expansion of your computer's RAM) kept hidden. Note, too, that there is an *hda1* partition. This is a Windows partition—the *vfat* next to the partition number tells us it uses the Windows FAT system.

The *ext3* file system used by MEPIS Linux differs from FAT in many ways, but the most obvious one is that if power to your computer is removed or you turn it off without going through the "correct" shutdown procedure, you can start it right up again without any problems. This is a feature even the latest versions of Windows don't have.

One last trick with the MEPIS Linux file system: It stores all your personal data in a /home partition by default—and not just your photos, text and music, but things like your favorite Web site bookmarks, your email, and even your desktop settings and other customizations, so you can easily upgrade or even reinstall MEPIS Linux without having to do a lot of setup or data restoration afterwards.

Now we get to the hairy part: actually partitioning our hard drive.

Right now we're at the Install screen, getting asked how we want to do our install.

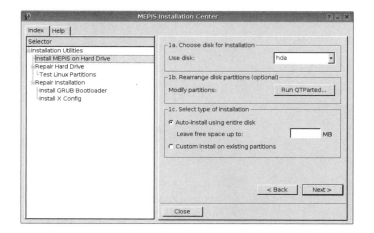

We choose Custom Partitioning. This brings up the QParted utility.

We click on *hda* to work with our one hard drive. (QParted allows for multiple hard drives. This is why we must click on the one we're interested in changing—even if the PC we're using as an example here only has one.)

We can now see the one big Windows (FAT) partition. To shrink it, we "grab" the

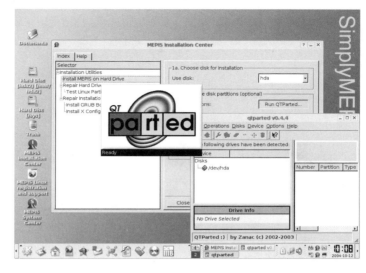

right end and move it to the left, which makes it smaller. The screen gives us a minimum amount of space we must allow. It's good to allow at least 20% more than this, and 50% more is better, just in case we need to add some more Windows files someday.

To actually make the change—at this point we can still change our minds—click on the little image of a floppy disk, which is the near-universal symbol for "save," except in QParted it's called "commit," which is more accurate here because when we commit to changing a partition we can't undo our decision. So let's do it and get it over with.

Now we have a large unassigned space to the right of the Windows partition. This is where we're going to install Linux.

We want to make three Linux partitions. The first one, called *mount*, is where all our programs will go. Select *ext3* as the partition type. We want this partition to be at least 3GB, possibly as big as 5GB. Then we *commit*. Next, we add a

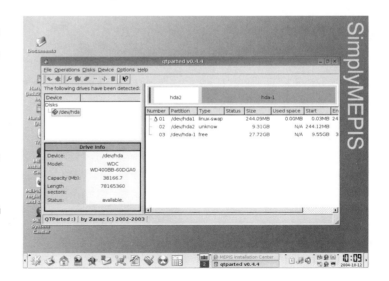

small partition type called *swap*, which acts as additional RAM memory in case we use up all our "real" RAM. This partition should be about as large as the amount of RAM memory we have, although this is not critical. Make it 512MB (*MB*, not *GB*), and you'll be fine. Our third partition is also *ext3*, and it's our *home* partition.

Our hard drive is now split down the middle, half for Windows and half for Linux. We're done partitioning.

Installing Linux by Itself

Let's go back a few steps to where we were asked what kind of install we wanted. If we want to install Linux all by itself on our hard drive, all we need to do is select "Auto-install using entire disc" and go from there. Much easier!

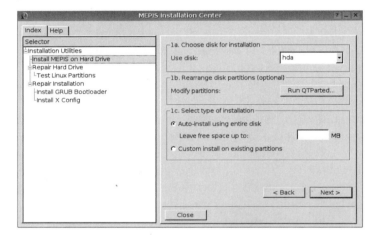

After we make this selection and click "Next," all we need to do is sit back and watch as MEPIS automatically formats our hard disc and installs itself.

The little bar will crawl across the screen as MEPIS installs. This is going to take between five and 30 minutes, depending on your PC's speed. Now is a great time to get up, stretch, grab a cup of coffee or a glass of soda, juice or water.

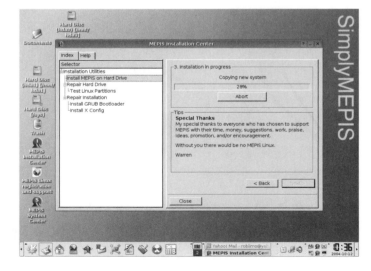

Names and Passwords

The next human intervention required for your MEPIS installation is saying "Yes" when you're asked if it's okay to install the GRUB (GRand Unified Bootloader) utility in the MBR (Master Boot Record). Go ahead; if you're an advanced Linux user you can customize your MBR later. The rest of us will be satisfied with plain-jane GRUB. It allows us to boot Linux in more ways than most of us ever need and gives us the ability to boot multiple operating systems, like Windows and Linux next to each other—or even two or three different Linux installations, if we like.

Our next task is deciding on a user name, a root password, and—if your computer is part of local network—typing in the network's name and giving your computer a name that will identify it to other computers on the network.

The user name can be anything you like. You can add more users later. Both the user and root passwords ideally should be a mix of numbers and letters at least six characters long, rather than a relatives name or something else that can be figured out by a lucky guess.

The root password is important!

The root password is one of the most critical pieces of information you need to put in while installing your new MEPIS Linux system. If you know your system's root password you can change user names and passwords later, but if you don't remember your root password you can't change anything important without going to the trouble of installing everything all over again.

The root password is your main line of defense against malicious hackers. You want to make it very hard, ideally impossible, to guess, hopefully by using a long string of randomly mixed letters and numbers along the lines of *32x49rtgwo5567*. The problem with this kind of hard-to-crack password is that unless you have an excellent memory, you are going to forget it, so you'll need to write it down somewhere. Then you need to make sure the paper you wrote it on is hidden from prying eyes.

So maybe you choose a less exotic password. At least make sure it's not a real word. And throwing a number or two in the middle can't hurt. That ought to be secure enough for non-government work. Just make sure you don't use this password on a Web site or someplace else it might be revealed to the rest of the world by mistake.

You only need to use your root password when you install or delete software, add or delete users, or otherwise alter your computer in some way. You won't use it every day. If you go the "write it down" route, it's better than forgetting it—assuming that you don't forget where you hid the paper you wrote it on, as this book's author did with a root password several years ago…

There are only a few more MEPIS installation screens. The first one is for SAMBA networking with Windows computers on a network. This can be set up later, and more details will be covered in this book's "Beyond the Basics" section. For now, just click "Next." The final screen is for security and dialup. Those who use dialup Internet connections will find full instructions on how to set them up in Chapter 5, "KPPP— Easy Modem Dialer Application." And on the security front, MEPIS automatically sets up a Guarddog firewall utility, and you should have a firewall on any computer you attach to the Internet, no matter what operating system it runs, so just click "Next" here instead of changing anything.

Your installation is finished. Time to reboot.

That's it. You're done. Your next move is to boot your new MEPIS Linux installation for the first time. Depending on your hardware, the LiveCD may or may not eject automatically. If not, you'll need to eject it manually while your computer is doing its startup routine. You may or may not need to change your BIOS settings if you changed them to get your computer to boot from the CD drive. (This depends on your computer's make and model.) In any case, you're ready to run Linux from your hard drive for the first time.

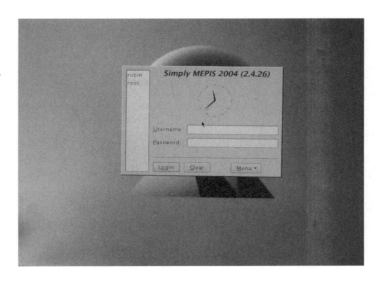

Your first startup is going to take a little extra time because your computer will now automatically run a utility program that checks your hard drive for flaws or bad spots and automatically moves critical program elements away from bad spots to good ones. This takes a minute or two, depending on your computer and hard drive's running speed, but as soon as this is done you'll see a login screen that gives you a choice between logging in as root or as the user you created. Choose to log in as the user, not as root, for security reasons.

You may want to briefly test your root login to make sure the password works correctly, but it's wise to disconnect your computer from the Internet while you do this—and go back to your user login before you reconnect.

But that's it. You have MEPIS Linux running. It's time to start using the applications software that was automatically installed along with it.

Section II

Linux Applications

Chapter 5

KPPP: Easy Modem Dialer Application

Most major Internet Service Providers (ISPs) work fine with Linux. A few do not formally "support" Linux—they don't want you to call them for advice about making your Linux computer work correctly—but you can dial into their phone lines with your Linux computer and connect to the Internet through them, without ever having a problem.

The easiest way to tell if an ISP is Linux-compatible is by whether or not it requires you to install special software on your computer to connect to its lines. If it requires special software, the service usually cannot be used with Linux. The most notable offender is AOL, which you cannot use without AOL software on your computer, and there is no Linux version of AOL's software. There is some irony here because AOL itself uses Linux heavily for internal purposes, but that's their problem, not ours. We simply accept the fact that AOL does not welcome Linux users, so we use any one of the thousands of other ISPs that do—and because most of them charge less than AOL, we are happy to use them instead.

But just because an ISP *offers* dialup software doesn't necessarily mean that software is *required*. This book's author has used the well-known ISP, Mindspring, for many years. While Mindspring is happy to supply you with dialup software for Windows or Mac PCs, they are just as happy to have you connect to their service with the KPPP utility on your *SimplyMEPIS* CD, which is just as easy to set up as any other ISP dialup program.

(If you're not sure whether your current ISP or one you're thinking about using will work with Linux, call or email them. They'll have no problem telling you.)

You will need the following information from your ISP to set up KPPP:

1. Your username
2. Your password
3. Phone number

Every ISP gives you this information when you sign up, and if you don't have it handy you can email or call and they'll give it to you again.

Setting Up KPPP

Obviously, we want to choose "Configure." And the main thing we want to configure is "Accounts," so that's where we'll start by clicking "New."

That will give you a choice of "Wizard" and "Manual Setup." You can look at the "Wizard" screen, but it won't do you any good unless you're in a country listed there— and the U.S. isn't listed. If you're in one of the listed countries, the "Wizard" will give you an instant list of popular ISPs there and help you get an account if you don't have one already.

Those of us in unlisted countries can use "Manual Setup" with no sweat, though. All we're really doing is entering our ISP name and local dialup phone number. Not hard!

Note that there's an "Add" button. Use this to put in the ISP's phone number. You can put in more than one number—a good idea in case one is sometimes busy or doesn't work—by using the "Add" button more than once (assuming your ISP has multiple local phone numbers where you live.)

You almost certainly won't need to worry about "Authentication." If you try to connect to your ISP and fail after you get everything set up, it may need to be reset, but this is rare, and it's something you can call your ISP to check on if you have trouble getting logged in. But we won't worry about this now. We'll just make sure we've put in a name and phone number for this connection and click "OK."

Ready to Connect

The only thing left is to type in your ISP username and password. After you've done that, make sure your modem is correctly connected to the telephone line and click "Connect."

One of three things will now happen. The most likely is that you'll uneventfully dial your ISP, get logged on automatically, and do whatever you want to do online. Your connection performance will be neither better nor worse using KPPP in Linux than with any other program in any other operating system.

The second most-likely event is that your modem will dial correctly but that the login will fail, leaving you with a "Disconnect" notice that includes some numbers programmer may find useful but mean little or nothing to the rest of us. If this happens, the most common cause is a typo in your username or password. Retype them and try again, and everything should now be fine.

The third problem, which happens with about five percent of all modems, is that you have a "Winmodem" that is simply not compatible with Linux or Mac or any other operating system other than Windows. MEPIS Linux will detect and automatically configure most Winmodems, but not all. There are ways to make almost any Winmodem work with Linux, but it's a lot easier—and a lot cheaper, if your time has any value at all—to simply buy and plug in a Linux-compatible external "hardware" modem if you have a desktop or a PCMCIA (card) modem if you have a laptop. (You can, of course, use a regular external modem with a laptop, but it's less portable and convenient than a modem specifically designed for laptop use.)

Troubleshooting Modem Connection Problems

The first thing to do when trying to figure out why a modem won't connect under KPPP and Linux is to listen to it. If you hear nothing when you're dialing your ISP, click "Configure" on the dialup screen and select the "Modem" tab.

Adjust the volume control in the middle of the screen. Modem speakers on PCs vary; one might be too loud when set to the default volume while another might be so soft at that setting that you can't hear it at all. If yours is too soft to hear, crank it up.

As long as we're on this screen, let's click the "Query Modem" button. If we get a list of results—that is, it looks like something's happening—chances are the modem is fine and any connection problems are unrelated to your modem and Linux. (Checking the cord connecting your modem to the phone line is a good idea; bad connections between the computer and phone system are a common cause of modem difficulties.)

If, instead of getting a series of little bars and other "I'm doing something" indications when you "Query Modem," you get something like "Cannot Detect Modem" or "The Modem is Busy," you will want to reboot your computer to make sure everything is working right. If that doesn't work, you probably have a Windows-only "Winmodem" and it's time to think about buying a "hardware modem" that doesn't depend on a specific operating system to run properly.

Modem buying hints

A Winmodem's packaging or online sales blurbs will list the Windows versions required to run it and will list *nothing but* Windows variants. A modem that also works with Mac OS or DOS is not a Winmodem, by definition, and will virtually always work with Linux even if its manufacturer doesn't explicitly say it will. Better yet, a search on Google or another search engine for the words "Linux modem" will bring up plenty of low-cost modems that will absolutely, positively work with Linux. Get a USB or serial port external modem, and you won't even need to install it. Just plug it in, and you're ready to connect.

A modem that dials, and that you can actually *hear* dialing, is a working modem. If you got an annoying "KPPD Daemon died unexpectedly" notice or something similar when you were expecting to see a notice that you were connect- ed and your username and password were accepted, the problem is probably not with your

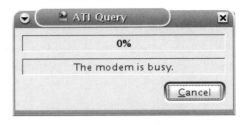

modem or software. The most likely reason for this problem is, as mentioned previously, an incorrect username or password. A second possibility is the "Authentication" protocol. A few ISPs don't use the generic "PAP/CHAP" method, but require either strict PAP or strict CHAP. You don't need to know what these terms mean (although you can look them up through a search engine if you're curious), just that you may need to use one or the other.

This change is simple to make in KPPP. Go to your "Configure" screen, pick

"Accounts," choose "Edit" your account, and click the arrow to the right of "PAP/CHAP."

This will give you several choices, including both "PAP" and "CHAP" individually. Your ISP can tell you which one you should pick if this is an issue, or you might just try them both, one at a time; it takes less time to make this change than to dial an ISP's customer service line and deal with voice mail menus.

One last problem can keep you from connecting easily to an ISP, and it only happens with a tiny percentage of ISPs in the U.S. and a shrinking number in the rest of the world: a requirement that you enter a "Static IP," a "Gateway," and a "DNS IP Address" to use the service. Only ISPs with very old equipment still require these settings, and they require them no matter what operating system you use, so an ISP that uses them should readily give them to you if you ask. You probably already have them around as part of the signup infor- mation they gave you when you first started using their service.

To change these settings, you are again going to "Edit" your account, and choose the IP, Gateway, and DNS tabs as the parts to edit. You'll need to click "Static" or "Manual" to put in the numbers. And if an ISP says you must use their DNS (Domain Name Servers) while connected to them, you must not only type in theirs but also click the "Disable exist- ing DNS servers during connection" box in the "DNS" window.

You can have multiple connections in KPPP, each with its own setting. This is essential on a laptop if you travel a lot, but can also be useful if you have more than one home ISP dialup connection.

Get more help with modem connections at `http://www.mepis.org/forum`.

Chapter 6

Mozilla: Your Key to the Internet

E ven though KDE has a built-in Web browser and email client that many Linux users love, *SimplyMEPIS* creator Warren Woodford and this book's author decided that Mozilla is both better-known and easier to use for people trying Linux for the first time. Therefore, it's the Internet tool we'll talk about in the *Point & Click Linux*! book and video. You'll probably want to experiment with KDE's KMail and Konqueror browser at some point. You may also want to try the new, Mozilla-designed Firefox Web browser and Thunderbird email client or, for email, calendar and general "organizing" functions, the highly regarded Evolution system.

KMail and Konqueror are included on your *SimplyMEPIS* CD. There wasn't room to include Firefox, Thunderbird, and Evolution, but they're available for separate (free) download from the MEPIS servers and other Internet locations.

But right now, let's concentrate on Mozilla.

Obviously, at its heart, Mozilla is a Web browser. It

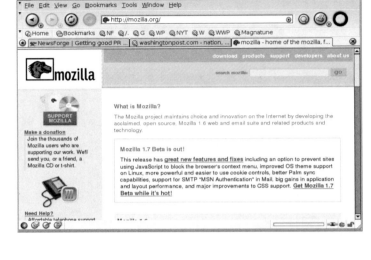

was originally an offshoot of Netscape, but is now far more advanced than either Netscape or Microsoft Internet Explorer. Indeed, many people who use Mozilla on Linux and are then forced to use Windows at work (or wherever) find that Mozilla is so much better than MSIE (as Explorer is called by many people in the Internet business) that they download and use the Windows version of Mozilla instead of going back to MSIE.

Mozilla's email client is another "star" compared to the primary competition. To begin with, it is immune to the popular email viruses and worms currently floating around the Internet. If you've been using Microsoft's Outlook or Outlook Express to read your email and worrying about viruses (as you should), the second you switch to Mozilla (or KMail or Evolution) that weight is lifted from you.

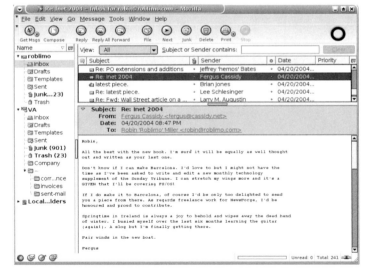

Someday, perhaps someone will write an email worm or virus that can spread to Linux computers through Mozilla, but no one has succeeded at it yet. You'll also enjoy Mozilla's built-in spam filter, which works at least as well as most of the ones for Outlook and Outlook Express that sell for as much as $50.

Mozilla also has an address book you can use as a contact manager and a *Composer* utility that you can use to make Web pages even if you don't know HTML.

In the following pages we'll show you how to use all of these functions, along with a few hints on how to make Mozilla look just the way you like it with custom themes and color schemes.

That should be more than enough to get you started.

More Mozilla Information:

```
www.mozillazine.org
forums.mozillanews.org
www.mozilla.org
```

Chapter 7

Setting Up and Using Mozilla Email

To use any email program, you need to know the following:

1. Your "inbound" mail server's name
2. Whether your mail server is "pop" or "imap"
3. Your "outbound" mail server's name
4. Your mail server username
5. Your password

Choosing an ISP

AOL, and a few other ISPs (Internet Service Providers) that require proprietary software installed on your computer to use their email service, won't work with Mozilla—or Linux.

If you currently use one of these ISPs, this might be a good time to think about changing providers. You can find reliable, Linux-compatible ISPs that charge as little as $10 per month.

We strongly advise you to shop for an ISP based on friends' and coworkers' recommendations, with Linux-friendliness evaluated only as an afterthought because the vast majority of ISPs (and almost all the most reliable ones) run Linux themselves, and are happy to have customers who run Linux.

Setting Up Email Accounts

When you start Mozilla email for the first time, it will automatically pop up an *Account Wizard* that will walk you through the process of setting up an email account. If you have more than one account, run the Wizard for each account. After you've got the first account set up, you get to the Wizard by selecting "Edit" from the choices along the top of a Mozilla email window, choosing "Mail & Newsgroup Account Settings" from the menu that choice pops up, then choosing "New Account" and going from there.

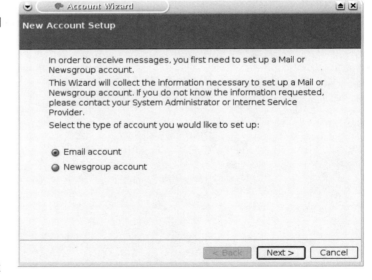

Either way, from the first Wizard screen on, it's just a matter of making simple choices and typing in basic information. The first choice is "Mail" or "Newsgroup." Yes, Mozilla can also read Usenet newsgroups, but those are not as popular as they were years ago, so we won't get deeply into that area right now—and most people who still like Usenet will have no trouble figuring out how to set Mozilla to read their favorite news-groups. So we're going to pick "Email Account" and click next, which takes us to this screen:

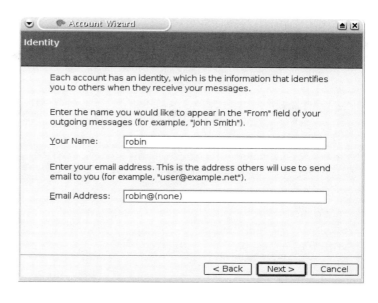

This is where we decide who we want the world to think we are. If our ISP gave us the account name "Frazzle12345" we can still have people send email to "Fred Razzle"—That's what goes in the "Your Name" blank. If we have a dozen email addresses and have one we'd rather have every-body use, we put it in the "Email Address" blank. (Most of us use our real names and email addresses here.) Then we click "Next" again, and get the "Server Information" screen.

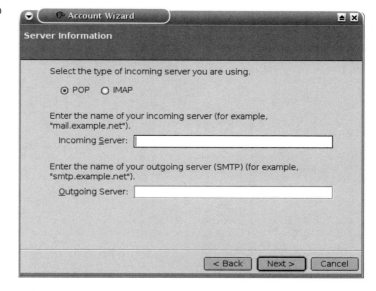

This is where we need some of the information we got from our ISP or network administrator. When given the "pop" or "imap" choice, if you don't know which one you have it's almost certainly "pop." The server name depends on how your provider has things set up. Just type in whatever they told you and you'll be fine. The same goes for the "Outgoing Server" space: Type in whatever your ISP or network admin told you should be there, and that's that. Next screen, please.

The name you type here is the one your ISP gave you, not your real name (unless they're the same). It could be something blah like "Miller123" or something colorful like "glowingsunflower" that you chose yourself. Either way, it goes here. Next:

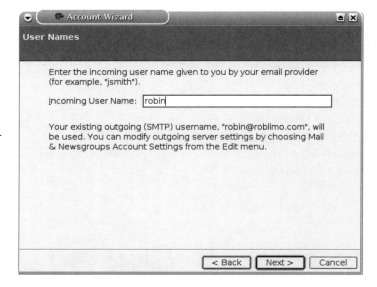

This is a "whatever you want it to be" choice, and is important only if you have more than one email account. You can type in "mail" or "booty call" or "mostly spam" or whatever else turns you on—even the bland "Home" or "'Work" choices suggested by Mozilla itself.

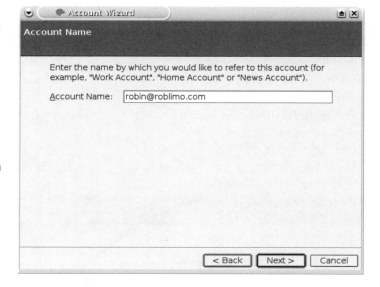

Note: Anything you type in now is easy to change later. Don't worry about making a mistake. The world won't come to an end if you do.

Hah! We're done, at least with this incoming mail account. Notice that this is our first opportunity to correct any mistakes we made by using the "Back" button to go back to our mistakes and redo them. If we have no mistakes (or after we correct any we spotted), we have only one last choice to make: Do we want to download messages now? This is up to you. Make that choice by checking or unchecking the little box, then click "Finish" and move on.

We're ready to download, read, and reply to our email, assuming that we set everything up properly. We'll need to type in our password the first time we access our email, but we only need to do it once on this computer; Mozilla can keep it for us and send it automatically.

This is a good time to send a "test" email to yourself to make sure that everything works. On a typical POP email server, it almost cer-

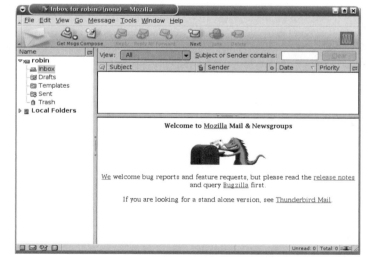

tainly will. If it doesn't work right on an IMAP server, your security settings probably need to be changed. Your ISP or company systems administrator can help you get them right.

Mozilla settings work exactly the same as Netscape settings, and they're the same in Linux as they are in Windows or Mac OS, so any competent ISP or corporate help desk person will know what to do.

Setting Up Mozilla Virus and Spam Filters

While Linux isn't affected by any Windows email viruses, we don't want them to fill our email inbox any more than we want spam to fill it, so we'll filter them out at the same time we filter spam and use the same tool for both: Mozilla's "Junk Mail Controls."

The "Junk Mail Controls" illustration shows the settings this book's author uses. They seem to give a good balance between eliminating "junk" and letting worth-

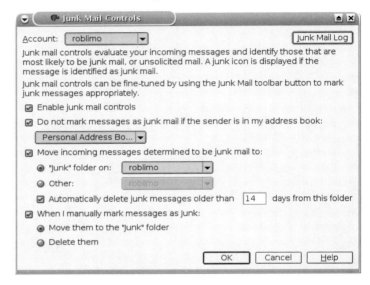

while messages through. You may want to simply duplicate them. But as we keep saying, your computer is your computer, and with Linux it's your choice how you want to handle things, not someone else's. Experiment. Try different settings. We'll give you a few hints in a moment, but first let's talk about how a Bayesian filter works.

One Person's Junk Is Another's Treasure

This is the secret of the Bayesian filter: It detects patterns in accord with your classification of emails as "junk" or "not junk."

If you keep tagging email with a particular string of words in it as junk, before long any email containing that string of words will go straight to the junk folder. If you go through the junk folder now and then—perhaps every few days at first—and reclassify some of the emails that got shunted there as "Not Junk," the filter won't classify future emails the considered similar as junk any longer. In other words, you train the filter according to your tastes instead of accepting someone else's definition of spam.

If you consign all your virus emails to junk world for a day or two, after that almost every one you get will go there automatically. With a little "tuning" by going through your junk folder a few times and marking anything that's there and shouldn't be "Not Junk," you'll soon have your junk filter doing a great job of screening your email for you.

Setting Up Email Folders and Filters

You can do many tricks with Mozilla mail beyond eliminating junk. One of the best is to automatically sort your email into many folders. There are several good reasons to do this. An obvious one is to keep professional and personal email separate. Another is to keep emails from each email list to which you've subscribed in its own file so you don't confuse one with another. And filtering your list email messages will also keep your junk mail controls from inadvertently classifying email list messages as junk, which is a common problem with all spam and junk mail filters, not just Mozilla's.

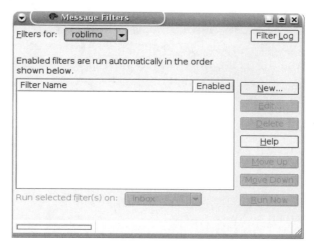

We get to the "Message Filters" control box by clicking "Tools" at the top of our Mozilla email screen and selecting "Message Filters" from the "Tools" menu. We create a new message filter by clicking "New."

Now we need to make decisions. Do we want to sort our messages based on subject lines, sender, the "To" field or what? And to what folders should we send which messages?

Here's a real life example: As a member of the Suncoast Linux User Group, this book's author participates in the SLUG (yes, we know it's a silly name) email list. The letters SLUG appear in the subject line of every SLUG list email, so we choose "Subject Contains" as our filter method. When we are asked what folder we want to send these filtered messages to, we click "New" and create a folder called "Lists" for all our email list email.

This is another action that's easier and faster to figure out by doing than by reading a description. Click on things and see what they do. If you make a mistake you can always "Edit" or "Delete" a filter you created, so there's no need to be afraid of making a wrong move.

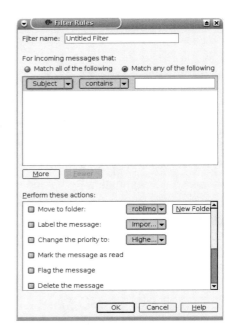

Now here's a fun trick: What if you subscribe to a number of lists? Or have six relatives who email you regularly, and you want to put all of their emails into a single "Family" folder? This is where the ability to "Edit" a filter comes in.

We only have two senders' addresses in this one. We can always add more later by clicking the "More"' button in the middle of the screen, but right now we'll click "OK" and move on.

Here's yet another fun trick: Whenever you run into an email you think ought to be filtered into a special folder, but you have no filter or folder for it, right-click on either the sender's address or the "To" address. You'll see several options, including "Add to Address Book" (which is a good idea if the sender is

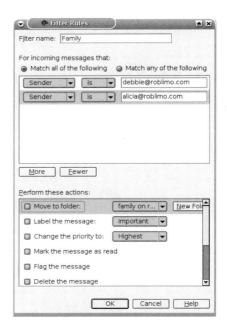

someone with whom you hope to enjoy future contact) and "Create Filter From Message," which will take you to the filter creation screens we just learned how to use.

More Mozilla Email Information

We now know what we need to know to perform

File Edit View Go Message Tools Window Help

most basic email tasks. We haven't covered some things that are too obvious to be worth mentioning, like clicking the printer icon to print an email. But there are a few other things we haven't covered yet that *are* important and *aren't* obvious. We're going to get to those now.

The most important thing you can do to teach yourself Mozilla mail's advanced features is to explore the menu choices at the top of the program window; not necessarily all at once, but a minute here and a minute there.

Some of the choices you'll find as you click on these little words relate to parts of Mozilla we haven't covered yet, but there's no harm in looking at them. By now, we hope you have enough confidence to explore without having your hand held every step of the way. So go ahead. Play around for a few minutes before turning to the next chapter.

Chapter 8

Mozilla Web Browser

U sing the Mozilla Web browser takes no training if you've ever used any other Web browser. You type in the address of the site you want to view, and there it is. If you click a link, you go to wherever the link leads. Click on a "Send Email" link and an email window appears. Click the "Print" icon and the page you're looking at prints out. Click the "X" in the browser's upper right-hand corner and the window closes. Select "File," click "Quit," and the entire browser shuts down. In other words, typical browser stuff.

What sets Mozilla apart from the most common proprietary browser, though, is that it can make your Web experience faster, easier, and more pleasant if you use its advanced features, which are advanced technically and in what they can do for you, but require no advanced knowledge to activate.

Let's start with tabbed browsing. This is something you don't know you need until you have it, but will never want to do without after it becomes a habit. To use it in its most basic form, when you click on a link, use your right mouse button and choose "Open New Tab" from the menu choices. This will open the new page in the same browser window but in a new tab.

"Okay," you say. "So what?"

Imagine you're looking for information at the Linux.com Web site.

You see an article you want to read, so you open it in a new tab:

If we'd just done our usual left mouse button click to open that new page and wanted to go back to the main page to check out articles, we'd have to reload it. But by opening the fresh page in a tab, we didn't move off the main page, so we can go back to it without waiting for it to load again. Now we can scroll down, spot another article we want to read, and open that new article in another tab, like this:

We can go on and on like this until we have so many tabs open that we can't read the writing on them because they're so crammed together.

Now we have 20 tabs open, and we could have more if we wanted. Try this with a search engine: Instead of clicking on one search result, going back to the search engine page, clicking on another listing, click-click-click open a whole bunch of them in new tabs. This is especially nice if your Internet connection is slow or you run into pages that don't load quickly or don't load at all. Instead of coming to a stop, you can read one page while the others load in the background. This is a huge advantage when you're doing any kind of research—and a huge convenience when you're reading news online.

Don't worry about opening too many Web pages

You can open a dozen windows, each for a favorite news Web site, and open ten or twenty tabs in each window. With Mozilla you can have a hundred or more Web pages open at the same time without any problem, and Linux won't crash under the load. It's an industrial-strength operating system, built like a truck to handle heavy-duty computing, and Mozilla is a heavy-duty browser that can handle nearly as much load as Linux. One of the things people who are used to other operating systems often have trouble understanding about Linux is just how rugged it is. Some people have gotten into the habit of only opening a few programs or browser windows so that their system is less likely to crash. With Linux this habit can safely be broken and you can use your computer like a draft horse, not like a prancing pony. Of course, after you're accustomed to using a strong operating system like Linux, it's going to be hard to go back to other, more delicate ones…

Managing Popup Ads

Mozilla can block popup Web ads for you. In fact, the first time one shows up after you start using Mozilla, you will be asked if you want to block popups, and will be led by the hand through the procedure for stopping them.

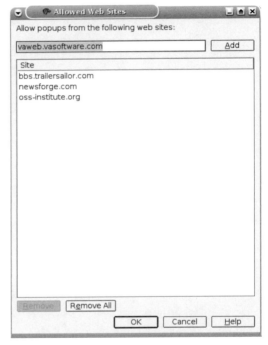

However, there are some Web pages that use popups to display illustrations (this is common on many shopping sites). If you run into one of these sites, click "Tools" at the top of the window, and select "Popup Manager." You'll see two choices. The easiest one, if you're currently on the site from which you want to accept popups, is "Allow Popups From This Site. "

Click "Add" next to the site address in the form space at the top of the window, then "Okay" at the bottom of the window, and popups on this site will be allowed in the future.

If you select "Manage Popups" instead of "Allow Popups From This Site" you'll get the same little screen but without a Web site address in the top form. You can type or paste one in if you like, or if you have a site from which you have been allowing popups but no longer wish to accept them, you can delete it from the list so that it can no longer give you popups.

Other Ways to Make Browsing Better

Mozilla has so many "Preferences" that it might take you days to explore and try out all of them. They're all optional, so you don't need to worry about setting them right away. But it's nice to know they're in there, especially since some of them can make the Internet a much better place to be than if you're using a less flexible browser.

Almost all Mozilla preferences are set through the "Edit" choice at the top of the browser window, specifically the "Preferences" screen you get if you click on the bottom selection in the "Edit" menu.

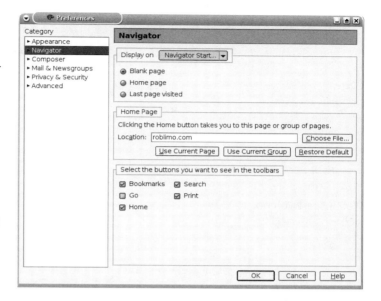

You'll notice that it's no big deal to change the page Mozilla displays when you first start the program. It can be anything you like—or if you choose "Blank Page"— nothing at all.

You can access other groups of settings by clicking on the little arrows in the left column of the "Preferences" window. When you click on those arrows they'll turn downwards and open up a new list of options, like this:

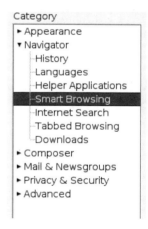

You don't need to worry about "Helper Applications" because the most popular ones are already included with the *SimplyMEPIS* CD that's part of this book, but the other areas this screen shows are worth exploring. For instance, the most convenient way to use "Tabbed Browsing" is usually to have the new pages load in the background while you read the one you're already on, but that is not the Mozilla default. You may want to change this. It only takes a single click.

Other "Navigator Preferences" are obvious if you look at the screens. For instance, you can change your search engine preference—the one you get when you click on "Search" just to the right of the form where you type URLs in a browser window—through the "Internet Search" screen, and again a simple click-click makes your change.

After exploring "Navigator Preferences," you ought to spend a few minutes checking out "Privacy and Security" and "Advanced" options, especially "Scripts and Plugins" under "Advanced."

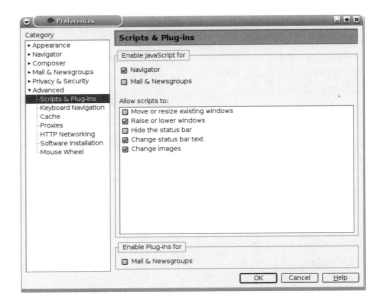

The most important button here is probably the "Move or Resize Windows" one. If you make sure this is *unchecked*, it will keep Web sites from taking control of your browser window and making it full-screen or oth-erwise changing it without your say-so. The other choices are less important; you will probably want to keep "Change Images" checked because many online slide shows rely on this javascript feature to work. The other choices won't affect most of your Web use. You can leave them alone and no harm will be done.

Other "Advanced" configuration options are nice to explore if you have time, but unless you're an advanced user they really aren't necessary.

Creating Bookmarks

Microsoft Internet Explorer (MSIE) calls them "Favorites," but "Bookmarks" is the original browser term for Web addresses you save so you can return to them later. Your *SimplyMEPIS* version of Mozilla comes with a number of preset bookmarks, but you can easily delete any you don't want and just as easily add your own. Many of the Mozilla screenshots in this book show the author's bookmarks, which are decidedly *not* the same ones chosen by *SimplyMEPIS* creator Warren Woodford. And in the Linux "it's all about choice" spirit, you are encouraged to create your own set that matches *your* taste.

The easiest way to make a new bookmark is to click "Bookmarks" in either of the two places it appears in the menus at the top of your browser window, and click "Bookmark This Page." This automatically adds the page you're on to the bookmark list you see whenever you click "Bookmarks." A slightly more sophisticated—and much more elegant—way to save bookmarks is to click "Bookmarks" and select "File Bookmark." Suddenly you have a lot more options, including a chance to put this bookmark on your "Personal Toolbar" next to the "Home" and "Bookmarks" buttons.

🏠Home 📖Bookmarks ⊘NF ⊘/. ⊘G ⊘WP ⊘NYT ⊘W ⊘WWP ⊘Magnatune

The "File Bookmark" dialog box is easy to understand. You already have the address and title for the page you want to bookmark—Mozilla picked them up automatically—and all you need to do is select a file where you want to keep that page. You can give it a shorter name if you like, especially if you're going to put a lot of page links on your Personal Toolbar. Just blank out the long name Mozilla automatically inserted in the "Name" space and type in one you like. In the case of

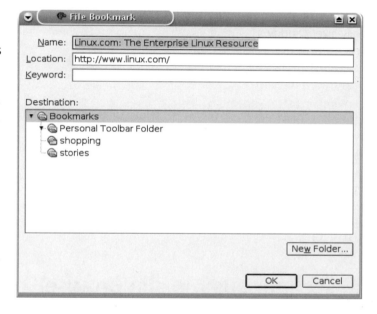

"Linux.com: The Enterprise Linux Resource,"' you might decide to call it simply Lc. Or "Linux." Then click on the "Personal Toolbar" choice and you're done.

You can add folders if you want to categorize your bookmarks. In the sample we show here, you see "Personal Toolbar," "shopping," and "stories." You click on whichever folder you want to use to store the page you're viewing, and its address goes there. Click "New Folder" and you create a new folder. Call it anything you like. And after you've created it, you can put all the bookmarks you want in it.

Going back to the "Bookmarks" button and the drop-down menu, there's also a "Manage Bookmarks" choice.

You can move bookmarks from file to file, delete them, even put folders within folders or add folders to your Personal Toolbar. You can rename folders and bookmarks, give them little descriptions, and give them special keywords to help you remember them—anything you want.

Alternately, you don't have to do any of this. It's all

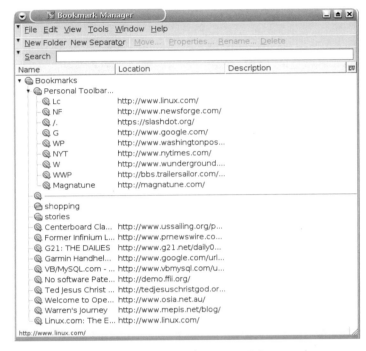

optional. But keeping well-organized bookmark folders can make your Web use a lot easier—and save a *lot* of time when you need to find a site in a hurry that you haven't used for months and which address you may have forgotten.

Miscellaneous Mozilla Browser Tips and Tricks

A great (and very simple) way to customize your Mozilla browser's look and feel is through the options in the "View" menu selection at the top of your browser window.

The "View Source" option is only of interest to Web developers who want to see a site's code, but some of the other options on that menu are important to the rest of us. The "Page Info" selection below it is a compendium of information about the page that you're viewing. It's worth checking out, but isn't generally useful for everyday Web browsing.

An *essential* item in the "View"' menu is "Text Zoom," which can immediately increase the font size on a site whose designer decided we should all squint to read tiny type. You can either use the click-on menu option or type "Ctrl +" to make type bigger. This is a great Mozilla feature. If your eyes are less than perfect you may end up using this one a lot.

Conversely, if you run into a site (usually an amateur one) that uses a giant font, you can "Unzoom" through the menu or type "Ctrl -" to make the type smaller.

"Show/Hide" is another great customization option. For instance, this book's author doesn't like the "Sidebar" that's standard in Mozilla because it takes up too much of his laptop's screen for his taste, so he's unchecked "Sidebar" to get rid of it.

You can also show (or not show) the various menus across the top of your browser window, depending on personal taste. This is a time for experimentation, not instruction; you can check or uncheck these all you like without hurting a thing, so go ahead and do whatever you like.

The one potential "gotcha" here is if you click "Full Screen." The method for undoing this is not obvious, so here it is: Next to the "X" in the upper right hand corner of the screen you'll see a little icon that seems to be a picture of computer monitors nested in each other. Click this, and your browser window will return to its normal size.

The last trick we'll discuss here is "Apply Themes." A number of volunteers have worked on ways to change Mozilla's appearance to match a wide variety of tastes. It is amazingly easy to download and install new themes. You have several to chose from in the Mozilla version included on this book's *SimplyMEPIS* CD, but there are many more available through the links you'll see if you click "Apply Themes," then select "Get New Themes."

Changing your browser's theme will not make it work any better, but sometimes it's worth a little extra effort to have software that not only *behaves* exactly as you want it to, but also *looks* the way you like best.

Chapter 9

Making Web Pages with Mozilla

This is a very brief introduction to Mozilla Composer; most of us don't make Web pages (or at least only make very simple ones), and those of you who are good at this kind of work will rapidly find your way around Composer without any hand-holding.

Composer is a simple WYSI-WYG (What You See Is What You Get) Web page design tool that takes no knowledge of HTML to use, although at least a *little* knowledge will help you turn out a better page. You use it much like a word processor by either typing in text or pasting in text you wrote in another word processor or text editor, adding pictures, then moving things around in the browser window until you

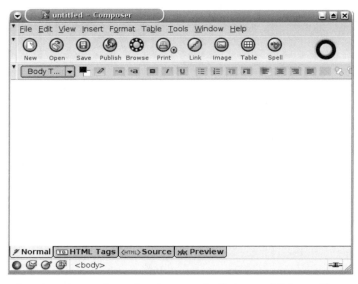

like the way everything looks, and saving the end result. There's a built-in "publish" utility that's supposed to help you send a page you made directly to a Web server, but it is of only limited use; you are better off using FTP if you are serious about Web publishing. Your *SimplyMEPIS* CD includes GFTP, a great (and very simple) FTP client.

Starting with a Blank Sheet of Pixels

Well, here we are with an uncreated Web page in front of us. We'll call it "Creating a Web Page about Mozilla Composer." We'll start by pasting in some copy we originally wrote in another program:

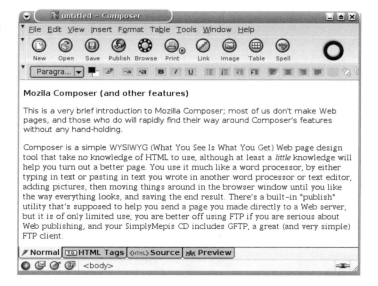

This is boring with nothing but unbroken text. Let's add a picture to it.

One of the toolbar icons says "Image," so we'll click on that one.

This is probably the nicest part of Mozilla Composer. With this tool you can easily resize and position your images. We aren't going to go into detail here because the instructions for this part of Mozilla are quite good, far better than most software instructions, and you can access them by clicking the "Help" button in the lower right hand corner of the "Image Properties" window.

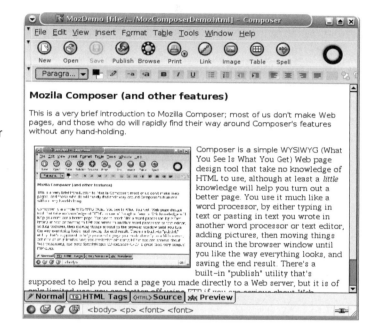

The "Help" habit

It's good to get into the habit of clicking on "Help" buttons and taking a glance at the instructions they display. Almost all the software included with *SimplyMEPIS* has those buttons on almost every screen, and while a few of them lead to scanty (or in a few cases no) information, the vast majority of them take you directly to pages that will actually help you. And Mozilla's documentation is among the best in the free software world.

Here's the page we just made, but with an image added to it:

As long as we were messing with it, we decided to make the headline one size bigger than in our original. It's easy to change font sizes with Composer; just look at the toolbar sitting on top of your creation, and you'll see several icons that obviously change text sizes and styles.

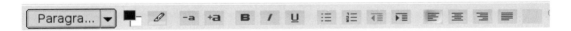

There are other icons on this toolbar, too. The one immediately to the right of the **U** (for underline) makes "unordered lists" with a big dot in front of each paragraph, and the one to its right makes *ordered* lists with a number in front of each paragraph. The next two icons respectively *unindent* and *indent* blocks of text, and the last four icons set your text flush left, centered, flush right or justified, depending on your taste.

To alter part of your text, just like in almost any word processor, you highlight the area you want to change by dragging your cursor over it while holding your left mouse button, then click on the icon representing the change you want to make.

Composer is a simple WYSIWYG (What You See Is What You Get) Web page design tool that take no knowledge of HTML to use, although at least a *little* knowledge will help you turn out a better page. You use it much like a word processor, by either typing in text or pasting in text you wrote in another word processor or text editor, adding pictures, then moving things

To change all the text on the page, you can either highlight it all with your cursor or go up to the top of your window, click "Edit," then choose "Select All"—or simply key in "Alt A" and get the same results.

> **Note:** The "Alt A" key combination used in Mozilla to "Select All" is not the same as the "Ctrl A" key combination used in almost every other word processor or text editor in the world to do the same thing. This is an annoying Mozilla quirk we hope will be eliminated in future versions, but for now we live with it—and because Mozilla is wonderful in so many ways, we will allow its developers this bit of silliness without getting angry at them.

Another important area you'll want to explore is the set of choices the "Format" menu button at the top of the page gives you. At the top of the menu, this button reveals you'll find several text choices that can liven up your page, and second from the bottom you'll see "Page Colors and Background," which allows you to change some colors and—if you wish—add a background image to your page.

The final "basic" Composer tool we'll look at is the link generator, which comes up when you click the "link"' icon in the tool menu we looked at earlier. To use this one, first highlight the text or picture you want to become a link, then click the icon. You'll get a little window with space to type or paste in the URL of the page to which you want to link.

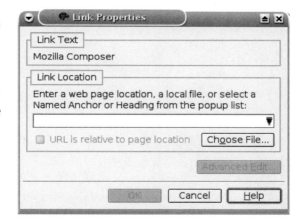

Make sure you include the complete link address, including the "http://" part. It's usually best to paste in a link from an open browser window instead of typing it by hand. This eliminates the possibility of a bad link cause by a typing mistake.

Composer can work with javascript, *Cascading Style Sheets* (CSS) and other "beyond HTML" Web-making tricks, but at heart it's a simple beast designed to help simple people (like us) turn out simple Web pages.

This book is obviously not a Web design manual. You should now have a basic understanding of how Mozilla Composer works. If you need to do more advanced Web design, no matter what operating system you use, you should delve into that as a separate subject with appropriate books and other material close at hand to help you learn this arcane art.

Chapter 10

Introduction to OpenOffice.org:
Word Processing, Spreadsheets, Slide Presentations, Graphics, and More

OpenOffice.org (OOo) is a huge, "all-in-one" set of office programs that has almost all the functions many people have gotten accustomed to using in Microsoft Office, plus some functions Microsoft Office lacks. It will open and edit most Microsoft Office documents, spreadsheets, and PowerPoint presentations competently; some formatting may get lost in complicated works, but you'll find that the actual content is intact.

You can also save work you create with OOo in Microsoft's formats, although after you realize that Microsoft formats take over twice as much hard drive space as OOo's "native" saving format, you'll probably only want to do this if you're sharing a piece you've created with a friend or coworker who only has Microsoft Office. In order to save hard drive space and hassles for both of you, it might be good to encourage Windows-locked friends to download and install a free copy of OOo for Windows from `www.openoffice.org`.

This introduction to OOo is just that: an introduction. OOo has so many features that it would take a book more than twice as large as this one to give detailed instructions on how to use them all. Today, we're interested in learning basic functions so that you can start doing basic work right away. This will still take a number of pages—enough that we have separate sub-chapters that cover each of several popular OOo functions—but not so many that you'll get lost. Besides, if you don't need to make or edit spreadsheets or create slide shows, you can skip those sub-chapters without worry and experiment with those areas later if you think knowing about them might be useful to you one day.

Get more OpenOffice help at

> `www.openoffice.org`
> `www.oooforum.org`
> `documentation.openoffice.org`

Chapter 11

OpenOffice.org Writer

OpenOffice.org Writer is your full-featured word processor, probably the most popular OOo function. To create a text document, type in some words. Basic formatting works about the same as in any other word processor. To save your work, click on the "File" option at the top of the screen and select "Save." You'll need to name your document. Unless you change where you want it saved from the default setting, it will go into a folder called "Documents" in your "home/you" directory.

You have a wide choice of formats you can use to save your work. The OOo native ".sxw" is usually best unless you're going to send this document to someone who only has Microsoft Office, in which case you'll probably want to use the extra hard drive space it takes to save it in Microsoft Word format. Or, if you're going to publish it on the Web, you may want to choose HTML. But you don't need to make this decision while you're still typing. It's good to save as you work "just in case," and you might as well use the standard OOo file format. You can always save your final version in a different file format later.

Save early, save often

Even though Linux and OOo are highly reliable, it's always a good idea to save your work as you go along. What if you wander away from the computer and a cat jumps on the keyboard or someone else starts pushing keys? You might get distracted and shut your computer off by mistake, or you might be using a laptop that runs out of battery power; or the power to your desktop might go off for a second. You never know.

Saving your work takes next to no time; hit "Ctrl+S" and everything you've written up until that moment will be saved to your hard drive.

The .sxw format OOo uses is just a fancy name for "Zipped XML," which means your work is first saved in the industry-standard "XML" format, then compressed using the industry-standard ".tar" protocol so that it takes up less hard drive space and makes for speedier email if you send your documents as email attachments.

If you need to open an OOo file without a copy of OpenOffice.org (or its commercial cousin, StarOffice) handy, you can "unzip" the file with almost any zip/unzip utility, in any operating system, and then read your text with almost any word processor, including Microsoft Word.

Another "Save" option in the OOo "File" menu isn't called "Save," but "Export." At this writing, the only format to which you can "Export" is PDF, and you can get the same result by clicking the "Export to PDF" line just below the "Export" choice. Presumably, there will be other "Export"' choices in the future, which is why there's a separate "Export" choice with room of other to-be-included formats, but for the moment PDF is fantastic enough. PDF, the "Portable Document Format" from Adobe, is the preferred format for many online documents that may be printed out by users, as well as in other situations where documents must look the same whether they are on a computer screen or paper.

Because PDF documents cannot be easily altered or have sections copied by readers, many copyright holders like to distribute their most valuable work this way. Many government agencies and academic institutions that want people to see *exactly* what they wrote, with line numbers and footnotes in the same place every time (which may not happen with HTML or other document formats), also prefer PDF.

Microsoft Word and Office don't save to PDF without special "add-on" programs. This, alone, is a good reason to start using OOo as your primary word processor and to encourage friends and coworkers to use it as well.

Adding Pictures to OOo Documents

At the top of your OOo screen, you have a typical list of choices you can click to bring down menus: "File—Edit—View—Insert—Format—Tools—Windows—Help."

"Insert" is your key here, specifically "Graphics"' from the menu you see when you click "Insert." There's a "Scan" option that will take a graphic directly from a scanner, but "From File" is a more common choice. This brings up a list of hinkty-looking arrows and other symbols and displays them so much larger than they should be printed that they look awful.

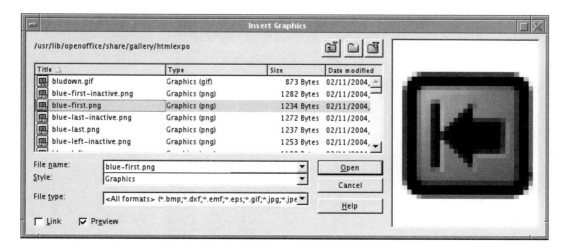

You can shrink these images so they look decent. In fact, you can shrink, expand, or change the dimension of any image you want to put into an OOo document, but first let's find a better image to put into one of our text files. Here's a nice one from our home/you/pictures folder:

If you don't remember how to navigate your file system, go back to Chapter 3, "Working with Linux: KDE and KWrite."

Here's that picture added to some text:

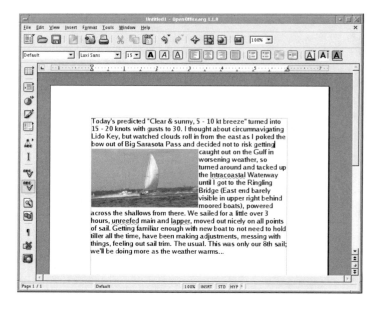

The way we got from the large image to one the right size for our page was through this screen:

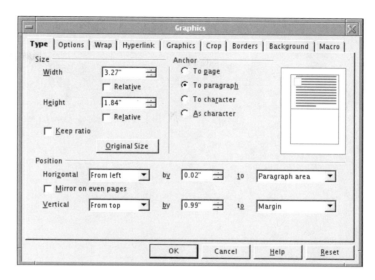

We got the "Graphics Control" screen by first clicking on the picture, which "focused" us on the photo. We knew we were focused on the photo because it suddenly grew little green squares at its edges. Then, after we were "on" the photo, we clicked again to see the many things we could do *to* it. This isn't a course in graphics handling, so we won't give you a lot of instructions here. Besides, it's easier and faster to grab a picture and click on this and that to see what happens than it is to *read* about it. You can't hurt anything if you click around here; in the end, after you're done playing with your document and any pictures you put in it, you can exit OOo without saving what you've done, and your test will disappear forever.

Of course, photos are not the only graphics you can add to OOo text. Charts and icons are just as easy to drop in and resize. If you want to move any graphic around on a page until it looks just right, all you need to do is grab one of the little green "handles" that pop up when you click on it and move it where you want. If you decide the new location doesn't look right, you can go to the top of the screen, click on "Edit," and click on the top menu item —("Undo") or just click "Ctrl+Z" to do the same thing if, say, you

used the little handles to move this picture of a tortoise to the wrong place on the page:

Welcome to OpenOffice.org Writer Help

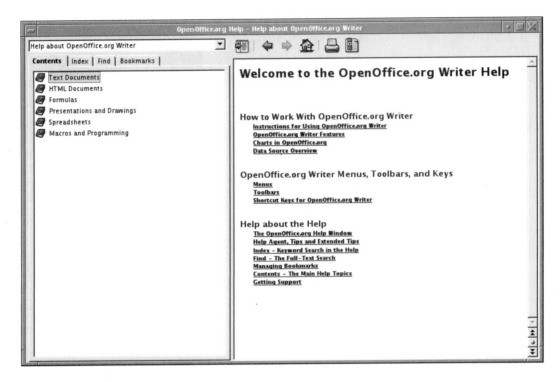

Each section of OOo has its own book-length "Help" manual that will teach you more than you need to know. You can read it all if you have time, but it is probably more efficient to use it as an index and look up how to do specific things as you need to do them. No one user is going to use all the features in a program the size of OOo, and no two users are going to use the same features. Some people will want to use OOo to put together two-column newsletters (and send them to the printer as PDF files, which printers like), while another may never turn out a paper newsletter but will want to use OOo to produce business cards.

Printing with OOo Writer

We got your printer set up in Chapter 2, "Running the *SimplyMEPIS* CD." To print your document, click on the Printer icon. It prints. If you want to set your printer to do more than just turn out pages in reverse order, choose the "File" menu (top left corner of your screen), then "Printer Settings" and change whatever you like. It's best to try doing this with a two-page piece first, not with a 100-pager, so you don't waste a lot of paper and ink experimenting.

You do, however, want to explore your printer settings with at least two pages, not just a single page, because some of those settings involve how pages are ordered.

Another trick you'll want to use some of the time, especially with complicated, multi-page printing projects, is the "Page Preview" selection from that same File menu, which will show you exactly how your printed page will look before you commit it to paper. This is especially valuable when you're making something like a two-column newsletter full of illustrations.

Yes, with some practice you can teach yourself to turn out reasonably complicated desktop publishing projects with OOo. It's an amazing program—especially considering the price— that can handle far more than basic office functions if you're willing to go beyond the raw basics of how to use it.

You don't always need a word processor

Some of this book's early chapters were written with a text/HTML editor called Bluefish. OpenOffice.org only came into play when the editing process started. That was when the collaborative editing features in OOo were needed in order to work with the publisher's production people, who use Microsoft Word, but it was easier to type early drafts as unformatted text.

KWrite is probably easier than Bluefish for most Linux beginners to use as a basic text editor; Bluefish is a tool that was designed for online writers and doesn't have a "print" function, which is why KWrite is part of the *SimplyMepis* CD and Bluefish isn't. The CD does, however, include the highly regarded HTML editor, Quanta+. You may find KWrite or Quanta+ better than OOo or other "heavy" word processors for everyday note-taking, simple writing, and producing material that's going to be published on the WWW instead of on paper.

Word processors are generally lousy for making Web pages. Neither OOo nor Microsoft Word turns out good HTML. Even Microsoft FrontPage does a poor job of it. If you are creating Web pages, you are always better off using a program designed for that task—like Mozilla Composer—instead of using a word processor.

When you write basic, unadorned text it's easy to add fancy formatting and colors later, but if you write them in at the beginning it's not always easy to remove them, no matter what operating system or software you use.

I'll show you how to get Bluefish and add it to your computer with a couple of mouse clicks—along with thousands of other free programs—in Chapter 24, "Downloading and Installing Software." There are dozens of text and HTML editors for Linux. Just because I prefer Bluefish doesn't mean you won't like another one better. Always remember, part of the joy of Linux is choice: with Linux, you can set up your computer exactly the way *you* want it. You are never stuck with someone else's choices.

Other Cool OpenOffice.org Writer Tools

Look at the menu at the top of your OOo screen. One of the choices is "Tools." Click on it and you'll see "Spellcheck" on top. You can have Spellcheck on all the time, underlining words as you go—AutoSpellcheck—or you can run Spellcheck on the whole file after you've written it. There's also a Thesaurus that will suggest alternate words if you find your imagination running a little dry and you think you've been using "however" (or whatever) too often. Also under "Tools" you'll find Word Count—an essential feature for writers who get paid by the word—and other useful utilities.

Some of these tools have icons to the left of your main working screen. Put your cursor over an icon and you'll get a bit of text that tells what it does. Click your left mouse button on that icon and you'll open whatever function it represents. Click it with your right mouse button and you'll have a chance to delete that icon if you think you're unlikely to use that function often, and you can also add icons for functions you use often but aren't shown in that right-side toolbar.

You might want to try adding the "Thesaurus" icon; it's not there by default, but it's awfully useful to have handy.

Chapter 12

OpenOffice.org Presenter

"**B**ut you can't do PowerPoint in Linux!" is often given as a reason not to give up Windows and its problems. This is technically a true statement, since "PowerPoint" is a Microsoft trademark, but you can certainly do slide presentations in Linux using OpenOffice.org Presenter. You can also use OOo to view and edit PowerPoint slides—and even save presentations you create with OOo in PowerPoint format so that Windows-using associates can play them back on their machines.

The first step in creating a presentation with OOo is to click on the "seagull" icon in the control panel at the bottom of your computer screen. From the menu this brings up, choose "Impress." That gives you a utility that guides you through the process of creating a (hopefully) impressive presentation.

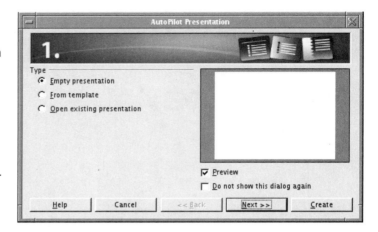

There are "Autopilots" for all OOo functions; these are essentially templates that take most of the work out of formatting a document, spreadsheet or presentation. Most people we've watched creating documents don't use the Autopilot function unless they've created their own custom document templates, a topic covered quite well in the "Help" index mentioned earlier, but Autopilot is helpful for graphically challenged folks (like this author) who need to create slides from time to time.

This is another moment when clicking on things to see what happens is easier than reading about what to click. If you don't like a choice you've made, click "Back" and make a different one. You can always change your slides later, anyway, so a mistake here is not crucial. In any case, after a few clicks you'll come to a screen that gives you a number of slide layout choices:

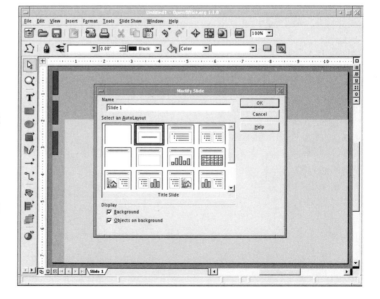

Talented artists can start with a blank screen and create their own; the rest of us are proba-bly better off—especially at first—using some of the built-in layout options. As you can see, there are plenty of them.

So we chose one, and you can see that it has simple instructions on it. To put in our own words, we click where it says "Click" and those words disappear so we can type in our own:

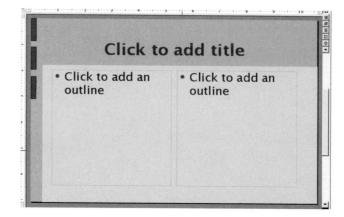

We can add more bullet points without thinking; a new one comes up every time we hit our "Enter" key, until our slide looks like this:

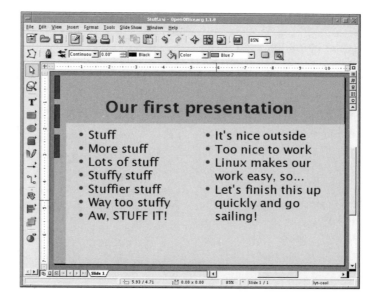

It's time to save this file and start making our next slide. We save our presentation the same way we save any other work we've done: Either with "Ctrl+S" or by clicking the "File" selection in the top left-hand corner of our screen and selecting "Save" from the menu. We can choose a file format, but for the moment it's best to use the default ".sxi" format; this is only our first slide, and we're going to make more.

We start our next slide by looking down at the bottom left of the slide we've just made. We see a little tab that says "Slide 1" and click to its right.

That gives us Slide 2, but we don't have to use the same layout.

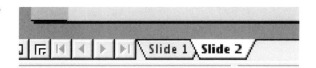

By clicking on the "Slide 2" Tab with our *right* mouse button, we bring up the same template selections we had earlier, and we can choose a new one. Maybe, because we've decided we'd rather go sailing, we'll choose a blank slide and fill it with a nice picture of a sailboat. We insert, place, and size the image exactly the same way we did in a "Writer" document, and we get a slide that looks like this:

We can add text over the image by clicking on the "T" to the left of our slide.

That will put a blinking black cursor right in the middle of our picture, but if we type a word or two, right-click on one of the words, and click "Text" on the menu that gives us, we'll get a new dialog box that lets us put the text where we want it—and do other things, like animate it if we're so inclined.

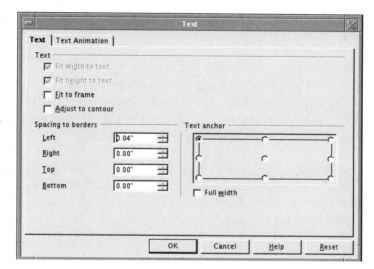

With text added, our number two slide now looks like this:

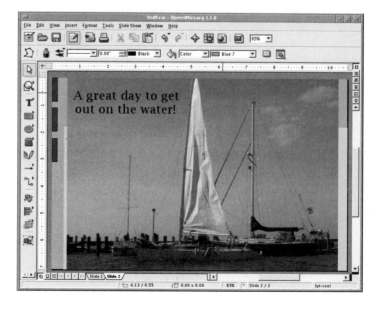

We can change text color, size, and general appearance by clicking on our friend the "Text" icon, highlighting the text by holding the left mouse button down while we pass our cursor over it, and selecting text changes from the row of buttons at the top edge of our working window:

We have many text options to choose from. Again, click around and try things. You can always do "Ctrl+Z"' or select "Undo" from the "Edit" menu if you don't like your last round of changes. Nothing is permanent until you do "Ctrl+S" or use the "File" menu to do a "Save" or "Save As"—and even then, you can open the file later and change everything if you have a sudden inspiration while you're out sailing.

You can now make all the slides you want by repeating the previous steps. After you get a few simple presentations under your belt, experiment with fancier ones. OOo will do all kinds of special effects, including animated transitions between slides. The sky and your imagination are the only limits.

Chapter 13

OpenOffice Draw

This is a simple program that won't do much for graphics professionals—or even skilled amateurs—but is useful for fast preparation of pictures you plan to use in OOo text documents or slide presentations. For "real" graphics work in Linux, we've included the GIMP (GNU Image Manipulation Program), an award-winning graphics program with so many features and plug-ins that we'll barely scratch their surface in Chapter 20, "The GIMP—Full-featured Graphics Application." But right now we're talking about OpenOffice.org, so let's use OOo Draw to get an image ready for publication in an OOo text document.

This is a picture of my assistant, Brice Burgess, taken while sailing at sunset on Sarasota Bay. It's a great sunset, but for publication we need to make this picture smaller and cut out most of the background. We open the photo the same way we open any other file, by selecting "File" from the menu at the top left corner of the OOo window, selecting "Open" from the choices available, and highlighting the file we want from the list we're given. (Remember, we discussed the file system in Chapter 2, "Running the *SimplyMEPIS* CD." If you don't remember how to use it, this is a good time to spend a minute reviewing those pages.)

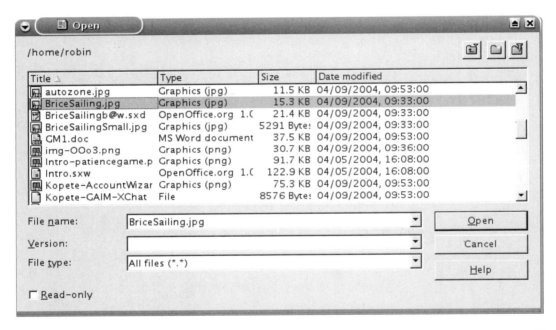

You'll see that the photo opened as part of a slide or text page, not as its own window. This is how OOo handles pictures—as part of something else, not all by themselves. To isolate the image so we can work with it, we click on it so that it grows little "handles" at its edges, like this:

As long as we see those handles, we are working only on the material inside them. In this case, we are going to make the photo smaller so it will take up less space on a printed page.

There are several ways we can do this. The most obvious is to lay our cursor on one of the corner handles and move it toward the opposite corner while holding our left mouse button. The only problem with this method is that it can distort the photo if we aren't careful, so we might end up with something like this:

This can be a fun "effect" if we do it on purpose, but this time we're going to either use the "Ctrl+Z" command or click "Edit" from the top Menu and pick "Undo" to take us back to where we were. Now we'll resize the photo correctly, by right-clicking on it, choosing "Position and Size" (the second menu choice from the top), and working with the dialog window that gives us:

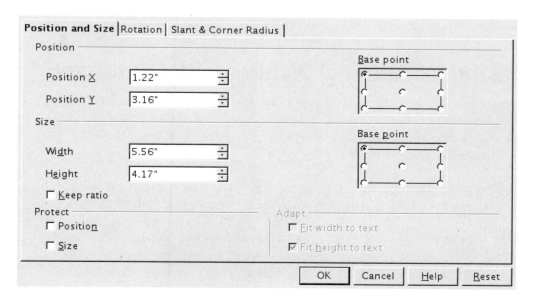

We can do a number of things with this dialog window, but right now we're just going to make our photo smaller. We can guess what size we want, in inches, and if we check the "Keep Ratio" button the program will automatically keep the photo the right shape if we change either its horizontal or vertical dimension.

107

We can also flip or rotate photos with OOo Draw. There are several ways to do it. One is to use the "Rotation" tab in that same "Position and Size" dialog window and either click one of the preset sideways, upside-down or 45 degree angle choices or use a little window to the left of the "big" choices to select your rotation angle in 15 degree increments. If those aren't enough choices, you can go to the menu at the top of the OOo window, choose "Rotate," and use

the corner "handles" on the picture to turn it, and try various angles until you find one you like. We happen to like Brice at this jaunty angle:

You may think this looks silly. No problem; remember that you can undo the change with Ctrl+Z or the Edit Menu "Undo" option, so you can have *your* Brice at any angle you want.

Making (or Altering) Pictures with OOo Draw

To create your own art, start with a blank drawing slate by clicking "File" in the top menu, then "New," then picking "Drawing" from the "What kind of new work?" choices that show up to the right of the main menu when your cursor is over (or to the right of) the word "New."

This gives you visible tools along the top and left side of your work area that are different from the ones you get when you open a "New Text Document" window.

On the left side of your work area you see a number of icons, starting with a pointer at the top. Each one will draw a shape or perform another function that will help you make a complete work of art. It would take thousands of words to describe in detail what each one does and how it works, whereas it only takes a few seconds to run your mouse over each icon and read the little text box that pops up. It only takes a few more seconds to try each one in the blank work space and see what it can do for you. Mistakes are fine. If you don't save your work after your practice, no one will know you made mistakes, and you will use no hard drive storage space preserving them for posterity. So, please, experiment freely. All pixels (the little dots that make pictures on your screen) created with Linux are fully recyclable; no precious resources or landfill space are needed during your self-training sessions.

As part of your exploration, check out the special toolbar that appears at the top of your work space when in "Draw"' mode, too. The toolbar on the left holds your "drawing tools," you might say, while the one on top changes those tools' characteristics. They're not well-marked, so you'll want to click on them a few times each until you understand what they do, which will only take a few seconds of hands-on trial and error. Bear in mind that an "error" here can be zapped out of existence with "Ctrl+Z"' or simply by not saving it, so it's fine to try anything you like, including using OOo Draw with your monitor or laptop upside down.

Saving Image Files

This is a spot where things get just a hair tricky, but it's *just a hair* so there's no need to worry. Remember how we said OOo treats images as part of a page or presentation? That's how it likes to save them, too. If you select the "File"' Menu choice, then click "Save As" while you're working with an image file, your choices will

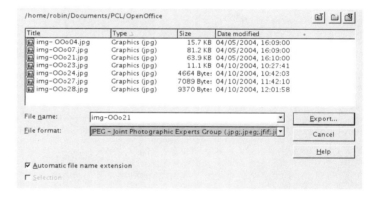

all be file types that only work with OpenOffice.org or its commercial cousin, StarOffice. They will not be image files that can be opened by all kinds of picture software and Web browsers and whatnot. So, being a hair tricky ourselves, if we plan to use an image file in anything other than an OpenOffice.org or StarOffice document or presentation, we "Export" it to the file format we want.

Instead of choosing "Save As" when we want to save our graphics file all by itself instead of as part of something else, we roll our mouse to four listings down the "File" menu and select "Export." That gives us a long list of file formats from which to choose. If you're an experienced artist or Web designer, you'll see most of your favorites there, even Macromedia Flash. If you don't know one graphics file format from another, the safest choice is JPEG. This is the format used by most digital cameras. Virtually all known graphics programs and Web browsers, for all operating systems, can read JPEG pictures.

There are only two more options we need to select if we decide to save the image in JPEG format: "Quality" and "Color resolution." Default quality is 75%, which is plenty good enough for Web publishing. But unless you're sure that this is all you are going to do with this graphic it's probably better to choose 100% because you can always *lower* the quality later, but once lowered you cannot *raise* it.

On the "Grayscale" versus "True Colors" choice, it's better to choose "True Colors" for much the same reason: You can always turn a color image into a black and white one later, but you can't add color back into one you save in black and white today.

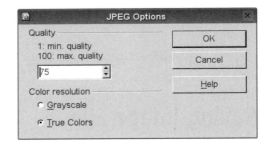

All we need to do now is pick a name for our file, decide which directory and folder are the best place to put it, and click "Save."

Chapter 14

OpenOffice.org Calc: Spreadsheets

I f you're accustomed to working with spreadsheets, this chapter will teach you how to work with them in OOo. If you don't use spreadsheets you may want to skip this chapter, and if you only use spreadsheets prepared by others and change them only by filling in blanks or making other minor alterations, a fast skim through these pages may be all you need.

As our introduction to OOo Calc, and to spreadsheets in general, we're going to create a simple chart showing a year's worth of sales for a hypothetical company that has five accounts, broken down month-by-month.

We start with a blank spreadsheet by selecting "File" from our top left menu in any OOo screen, then "New," then "Spreadsheet." That gives us a blank spreadsheet.

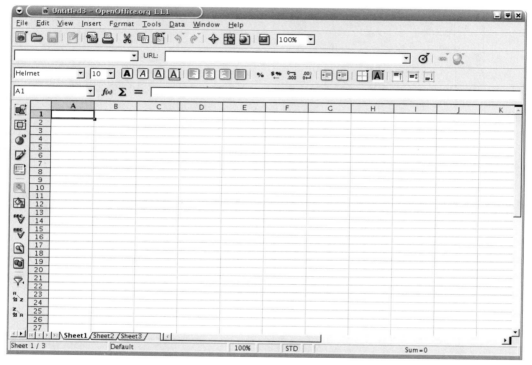

Note that our blank spaces are shown as "1,2,3..." going down, and "A, B,C..."' across the top. Each blank space has a location like "A1" or "B10." We're going to start by putting the months of the year across the top of the spreadsheet in A2, A3, and so on, up to A13. We're going to leave the "A" column blank because that's where our client names will go. And come to think of it, since some of our client names may be too wide to fit in that little blank, let's make the "A" column a lot wider before we do anything else.

We do this by putting our cursor on the line between two of the letters, in this case "A" and "B," which makes it suddenly grow two little arrow tips, one pointed

	A	B	C
1		January	
2			
3			
4			
5			

left and one pointed right. While holding our left mouse button, we move that line the direction we want it to go. In this case, since we want to make the "A" column wider, we drag that line to the right, probably to about where the line between "B" and "C" were when we started.

Now we have room for long company names and we can start typing them in, along with the months of the year.

There! We have the months typed in, along with some client names. We started our list of client names in row 2 instead of at the top in row 1, just as we started our list of months in column B instead of A, so that everything lines up neatly.

	A	B	C	D	E	F	G	H	I	J
1		January	February	March	April	May	June	July	August	Spetember
2	BangaDoods									
3	DelhiNoodles									
4	BombaySoftware									
5	BengalWorks									
6	OnshoreInsource, Inc.									
7										
8										
9										

Uh-oh. It looks like we spelled "September" wrong. There are two ways we can fix this. One is to use the built-in OOo spellchecker, which we bring up (in any OOo screen) by clicking "Tools" in our top-of-window menu, then selecting "Spellcheck," the top item on the list. (We can also get a spell check by

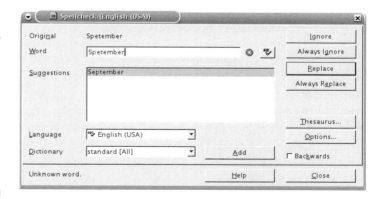

clicking the "ABC plus Checkmark" item on the menu along the left side of our window, or by just hitting our keyboard's "F7" key.)

113

The other way to correct that bad spelling, and an easy way to change information in a spreadsheet "cell" (which is the formal name for each of the little rectangles in your spreadsheet window), is to use the bar and form above the main window that appears only when you're running Calc.

Notice that above this bar you see your usual text options, the same as in OOo Writer. They work the same way in Calc. But the new bar is the one we're looking at right now. You can use the little form at the left to choose a cell by typing its location there, such as "L6," or you can choose a cell by just clicking on it in the main window. Whatever is in that cell will now appear in the large form space on the right side of this new toolbar, and you can edit it like any other piece of text—or enter brand-new material for that cell if there isn't already something in it. When you click "Enter," whatever you have typed is entered in your chosen cell.

Hey! We Just Made a Database!

So far, all we've done is enter data, essentially creating a "flat database." We can keep on with this, entering data about 5,000 or 50,000 customers and their purchasing histories, and if desired we can add additional cells with all kinds of other information about them, such as their addresses and phone numbers, plus names of our primary contacts within each company. If we have purchase order numbers we can add cells for those. We can enter any information we want or even create cells for information we don't need to enter now but might need to in the future.

We can then call up records in many ways by clicking on the appropriate cells. Do we remember that there's a guy named "Raji" we need to call, but don't remember his full name or what company he works for? We can go to "Contacts" by calling up just the column that has contact information for our customers and scanning it manually or sorting through the entries in that column by "sorting" the names in it by alphabetical order (or any other way we like) until we find our friend Raji. After we've found him it's simple to note his company and its phone number and call him. With a little practice (and some digging through the OOo "Help" pages) we can even look for things like partial phone numbers in badly scrawled telephone messages and find out who wants us to call them back.

At home, we could use this same tactic to sort through a huge recipe file looking for "brown rice" in an ingredient list if we have a sudden taste for a meal made with brown rice and want to see which recipes we have that use brown rice.

While OpenOffice.org Calc is not a true database, we can use it as one, either as its only function or in addition to its true function as a spreadsheet, which involves calculations of one kind or another—and is why it's called "Calc" instead of "Database" or "File."

Calculating with Calc

Let's be lazy. Instead of using an entire year's worth of sales information for our hypothetical customers, let's just use one quarter, or three months. This will save typing (and reading) in our example, and will teach us just as much.

> ### Big spreadsheets are just like small ones, only bigger
>
> Working with data covering large numbers of customers and many years of sales takes no more computer knowledge than working with a few sample customers and a few months' worth of sample data. So, whatever skills you learn here be useful when you become CEO of a worldwide corporation with millions of customers. You can sit on the deck of your yacht, using a spreadsheet running on your gold-plated laptop to decide how many thousands of employees you will lay off before your afternoon swim.

Here's our sample data. We're going to display the total sales to each client company in column "E" and average monthly sales in column "F."

	A	B	C	D	E
1		January	February	March	
2	BangaDoods	$31,243.00	$38,210.00	$26,459.00	
3	DelhiNoodles	$11,250.00	$10,500.00	$12,200.00	
4	BombaySoftware	$61,333.00	$74,992.00	$68,556.00	
5	BengalWorks	$24,980.00	$21,650.00	$34,967.00	
6	OnshoreInsource, Inc.	$4,200.00	$25.00	$28,459.00	

The command we use to create a total sales figure for one of these companies is

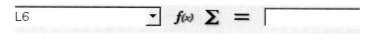

=SUM (B2:D2), and that's extremely arcane the first time we want to do it, so we let OOo guide us through the process by clicking on the *f(x)* symbol in our Calc toolbar.

That gives us a dialog box listing hundreds of ways we can manipulate or combine the numbers in our spreadsheet's cells.

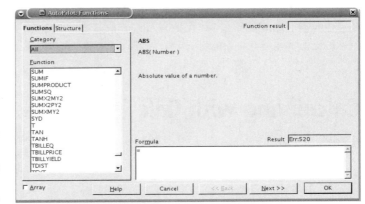

We choose "Sum" (way down the alphabetical list on the left side of this pop-up dialog screen) because all we want to do right now is simple addition, or a SUM. After that, click "Next" and choose which spreadsheet cells we want to add together.

Now we're on this slightly confusing screen in the dialog box:

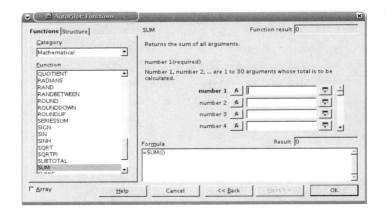

It's time for a little help, so we click the Help button.

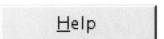

This opens the built-in OpenOffice.org manual to the page we need:

The language is arcane (because spreadsheets are arcane) but if we look for a moment we see this useful section:

Example:

If you enter the numbers 2; 3 and 4 in the Number 1; 2 and 3 text boxes, 9 will be returned as the result.

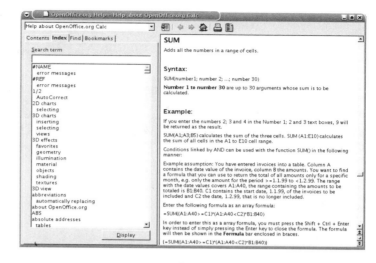

SUM(A1;A3;B5) calculates the sum of the three cells. SUM (A1:E10) calculates the sum of all cells in the A1 to E10 cell range.

Aha! We can either enter each of the cells we want to add manually, separated by semi-colons, or we can just enter the *first* cell and the *last* cell we want to add, with a colon between them, and automatically grab all cells between the two. This second choice is a lot easier than typing in a whole string of cell locations, especially when you're dealing with spreadsheets that have thousands of entries.

The OOo help files: always there for you

There's a rather complete manual built into OpenOffice.org. We mentioned earlier that you can access it from the "Help" listing in the menu at the top of every single OOo window. But OOo "Help" can be even more helpful than that. When you're doing almost anything in OOo, there's a "Help" button nearby that will take you directly to a manual section that relates to what you're doing (or trying to do).

OOo manual sections vary in quality, and most of them are written in a style only a computer programmer could love, but all the information you need is there if you read the relevant sections carefully.

An online tool that can help you understand the OOo manual (and computer manuals in general) is the *Webopedia* at `www.pcwebopedia.com`. One of the big problems with computer hardware and software manuals is that they assume you already know things most people don't know. *Webopedia* will help you translate programmer-speak into English.

We have made our little chart, and it looks like this:

	A	B	C	D	E	F
1	Customers	Jan	Feb	Mar	Total	Average/month
2	BangaDoods	$31,243.00	$38,210.00	$26,459.00	$95,912.00	$47,956.00
3	DelhiNoodles	$11,250.00	$10,500.00	$12,200.00	$33,950.00	$16,975.00
4	BombaySoftware	$61,333.00	$74,992.00	$68,556.00	$204,881.00	$102,440.50
5	BengalWorks	$24,980.00	$21,650.00	$34,967.00	$81,597.00	$40,798.50
6	OnshoreInsource, Inc.	$4,200.00	$25.00	$28,459.00	$32,684.00	$16,342.00
7						

We have our sales month-by-month, per customer, plus a total and average for each customer. We could add all kinds of other calculations (several books' worth) here, but we won't do that to you today. Instead, let's see how this little chart would look if we wanted to print it out. We do this by going to the top of our OOo window, selecting "File," and choosing the "Page Preview" choice. That gives us this page:

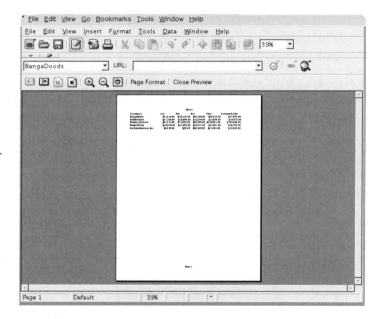

This is not a fancy chart. We could choose "Page Format" and jazz it up with colors and lines and even a picture as a background. (Go ahead. Poke around and play with these tricks. Knowing them might come in handy one day.) Or maybe we'd rather show it as a graphic bar chart or pie chart instead of as rows and columns of figures. We can do this, too.

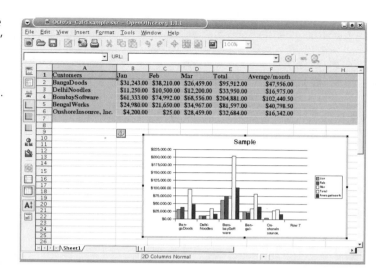

First we get rid of the "Page Preview"' view by clicking "Close Preview" on the preview page. Next, we go to the top-of-window menu and select "Insert," then select "Chart" from our list of choices. From there, it's basically a matter of following instructions and making choices. The first few times you try this, you will probably want to hit that magic "Help" button more than once, but after a while, like most people who use spreadsheets often, you'll find a few favorite chart styles and stick to them almost all of the time.

You Are Not a Spreadsheet Expert Yet

This has been nothing but a toe in the spreadsheet waters. If you are not accustomed to creating and modifying spreadsheets but need to become fully competent with them, you will need to study and practice for weeks or months, no matter what spreadsheet program you end up using most of the time. www.OpenOffice.org's "Support" section has a number of OOo "Calc" tutorials, and a quick trip to any major search engine will point you to many more.

Another way to learn is to simply try things out and see what happens, using that "Help" button whenever you run into a feature you don't understand. Learning on your own, at your own pace, is easier for many people. Although it won't look as good on a resume as formal classes, when you're on the job the knowledge gained through self-study is just as useful as knowledge you acquire through more formal channels.

Chapter 15

OpenOffice.org, Microsoft Office, and StarOffice

Despite the amazing growth of OpenOffice.org (OOo)—millions of new users every year—Microsoft Office is still the world's most popular general office software package. Indeed, one of the great "features" of OOo is that you can use it to open and work with Microsoft Office files. But don't expect 100% compatibility with MS Office. You won't get it. Instead, expect to get enough compatibility for everyday work, with some of the "frills" left out.

The biggest problems with translating MS Office files to OOo are formatting and scripts. The information (as in text or pictures) jumps the bridge without complaining, but a few "extras," like fancy animated slide transitions in PowerPoint, may get lost.

MS Office uses Microsoft's proprietary *Visual Basic* programming language to create most of the "macros" that produce fancy effects like slide transitions and automatic page formatting. There is a more-or-less equivalent language for OOo called *StarBasic* that is included with OOo, but it does not use the same commands as *Visual Basic*. Only Microsoft and Microsoft licensees are allowed to use *Visual Basic*. This is a problem for anyone who is not using Microsoft products, but not a large one—except for Microsoft, as a growing percentage of the world's computer users discover that *Java* and other computing languages can be used on many operating systems (including Linux) with software produced by companies not affiliated with Microsoft, and even with free software (like OOo), and will also work nicely with Microsoft operating systems and software.

But we live in the here and now, not in someday-land, and part of the price we pay in a Microsoft world for not using Microsoft products is slight losses in translation from Microsoft's file formats to others. In return we get other advantages, like the ability to use OOo to turn out PDF documents with a single click, not to mention cutting our software licensing costs down to nothing.

Consider StarOffice for Professional Use

StarOffice is OpenOffice.org's commercial cousin. It has more templates for documents and charts, more built-in clip art, and better tools for importing MS Office files. Its cost is still low compared to the competition (less than $80), and it's fully compatible with Linux—along with Windows and Solaris.

StarOffice includes a complete manual, 60 days of free phone support and a free Internet training course called "Transitioning to the StarOffice 7 Application Suite." These alone are worth its low price.

Free OpenOffice.org is probably all you'll ever need for home or school use, but in a professional environment, you may decide that StarOffice is worth the small additional investment.

Chapter 16

CheckBook Tracker— Simple Bookkeeping with Linux

CheckBook Tracker is a checkbook-based program suitable for home and small office use. Other, more advanced, accounting programs are available for Linux, including the excellent GnuCash system for classic double-entry bookkeeping, which you may decide to download and install once you get a little more comfortable with Linux. We're covering CheckBook Tracker for the *SimplyMEPIS* CD because it is easy to understand, imports the .qif files most Windows accounting programs use, and it works nicely with the *Open Financial Exchange* (OFX) file format used by most major banks' online banking systems.

Getting Started

When you open *CheckBook Tracker* (CBT), your first response might be, "Huh? Did it load correctly? There's nothing here."

Don't worry. It loaded correctly. Nothing appears because there's nothing there yet. Step one is to click on "File" and create a file of some sort so there *is* something to work on.

This gives us the same "file" window we've seen before, with the option of choosing in which folder we want to house our new file, and the space to type in the name of our new file. For this demo, we're putting the new file in our "home" directory, although it might be smarter to create a "finances" directory for neatness. For this demo we're calling our new (demo) file "home" because it's going to track home, not business, finances.

Now we have something to work with. Our first step is to enter a starting balance. For this demo, we entered $0.00. Now we'll make a deposit by clicking on the "Deposit" tab and choosing "New." We fill in the information requested, then click "OK" to enter it.

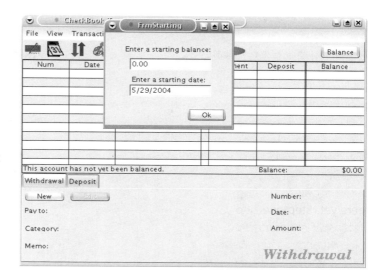

We now show $812.00. Let's spend some of it, because that's what money is for.

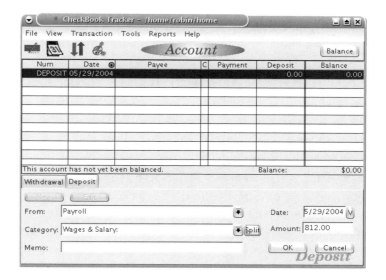

125

Both the "Deposit" and "Withdrawal" screens have long drop-down lists of categories from which money can come and to which it can go. If you need a category that's not already in the list, type the name you want it to have instead of using one of the existing ones and it will automatically be added to the list when you save your entry. In this example, we added the "West Wight Potter Book" category

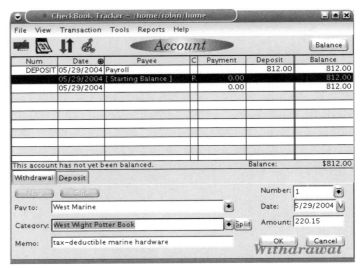

because we are going to write a book about our West Wight Potter, a small sailboat we own. Because we're writing that book, all our boat expenses are tax-deductible, so we note that in the "Memo" space.

Downloading Files from Your Bank

This book's author downloads checking account activity monthly using Bank of America's "WEB Connect for Quicken 2001 and above" option, then opens CheckBook Tracker and imports those files. Your bank may offer different download options, and you may choose to download your bank information and reconcile your account more often than once a month. Once every few months might be sufficient if you don't have a lot of banking activity. This is a case where you should experiment and decide what best suits your needs instead of being locked into someone else's preferences. The not-so-old saying, "You are unique, just like everyone else," applies here. There is no one-size-fits-all set of financial solutions. CheckBook Tracker is flexible enough and simple enough to set up and change that you can easily try different options until you have things the way *you* like them. This only takes a few minutes, and you only need to do it once.

Visual Reports

This is the fun part—unless your finances are in bad shape and you don't really want to see how you're doing in an easy-to-grasp visual format. Here are two popular CheckBook Tracker report styles:

Expenses by category:

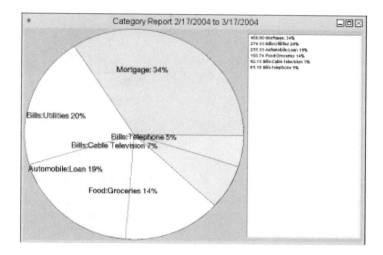

Balance History:

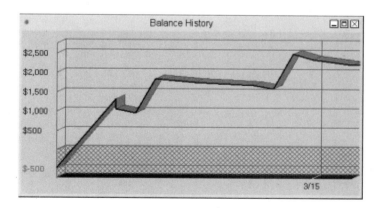

Printing Checks and Other Settings

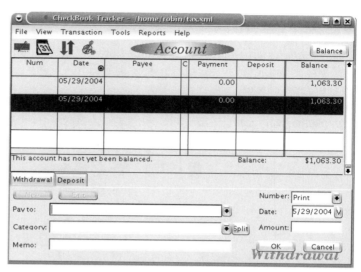

For those who don't yet do their bill-paying online, CheckBook Tracker will print checks based on standard "computer print" check forms available from your bank, office supply stores, or the "home office" sections of most discount stores.

To set up a printable check, go to the top of the CheckBook Tracker window, select "Transaction," then "New Print Check." Fill in the appropriate information (you can have check numbers increase automatically from where you last left off—or start with #1 if you like).

The ideal way to print checks is in batches, so you'll want to "write" all the checks you want to send today, load your printer with check blanks, click on "File" at the top of the CheckBook Tracker window, and hit "Print Checks."

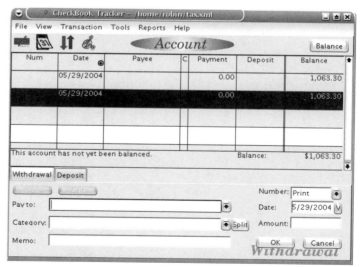

The first time you print checks with CheckBook Tracker (or any other check-printing program), it's a good idea to print a couple of "dummy" checks on blank paper first and hold them up to the light on top of a sheet of check blanks to make sure everything prints in the right place. Chances are, everything will work fine, but if you need to adjust anything, go to the top menu, select "Tools," then

"Settings," and click on the "Check Printing" tab. Here you can adjust exactly where every piece of information on your checks will print, in accordance with the instructions included with your preprinted check blanks.

While we're on the "Settings" screen, we might as well look around and check the rest of it. The defaults are fine, but you can always change things to suit your personal taste, including fonts, the way graphs display, and even sounds. Perhaps you have a little sound clip around of someone crying, and you'd like to have it play every time you make a withdrawal—and have the sound of applause play every time you make a deposit. (I'm not *advising* you to do this, but you can if you want.)

One last note: Of all the data on your computer, your financial information is probably the most important. You should back it up regularly. CheckBook Tracker will ask if you want to back up to a disk every time you close the program. Your answer should always be "yes." You can reuse the same disk over and over, so the cost of taking this precaution is so small you can barely measure it; however, the value of keeping a second set of your records is *huge* if your hard drive ever decides to stop working.

More CheckBook Tracker Information and Help:

The "Help" button on every CheckBook Tracker screen leads to "Contents," which displays the CheckBook Tracker manual in your Web browser.

The CheckBook Tracker "help" forum can be found at `tony.maro.net/mod.php?mod=forum&op=pick&forumid=2`.

Chapter17

Kopete: IM, IRC, and General Chat

K opete is an "all-in-one" tool that gives you access to AIM, ICQ, MSN, Yahoo! and other popular "online chat" services, plus Internet Relay Chat (IRC). It is simple to set up and configure. You can use it without any configuration beyond adding accounts with the simple account "wizard," but if you want to spend a few extra minutes, you can choose background colors, formats in which messages appear, and many other things that will make Kopete truly *yours*.

Set Up Kopete to Access AIM

We'll use AOL Instant Messenger (AIM) as an example, but the Kopete Setup Wizard works the same way with all popular chat services. The first time you open Kopete by clicking on the Kopete icon in the panel at the bottom of your screen, the "Signup Wizard" will open automatically.

The Wizard is just as "wizard-like" as you'd expect a setup wizard to be: You follow instructions, click "Next" when you finish with each screen until you come to the last one, and click "Finish" to save the username and password you've typed.

The Setup Wizard assumes that you already have an account on your chosen service (AIM in our example). If you don't, there's a link in the lower left corner of each signup screen that goes to the Web page where you can sign up for an account on that service, then come back and set Kopete to work with it.

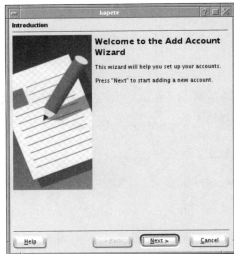

After you have AIM—or another service—set up, when you start Kopete you won't get a Setup Wizard automatically; to enter information for another account you click "Settings" at the top of the little Kopete window that pops up when you start the program, then select "Configure Kopete" at the bottom of the little menu the click on "Settings" brought to your screen.

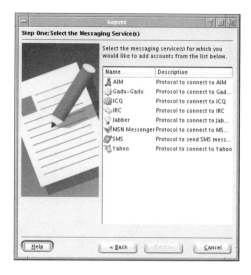

From this screen, pick "Accounts" and you'll see the AIM account you already set up. Click "New" on the right side of this little screen to bring up the Account Wizard, then "Next" to show a list of services to which Kopete can connect you—exactly the same as when you set up the AIM account, and all of them except Internet Relay Chat (IRC) are set up the same way.

133

The one other choice you might want to make when you're setting up instant messaging accounts in Kopete is to click the "Connection" tab you see peeking over the top of "Edit Account" screen when you click "Modify" after highlighting an account you've already set up. There's only one choice here: Do you want to log onto this service automatically every time you start Kopete?

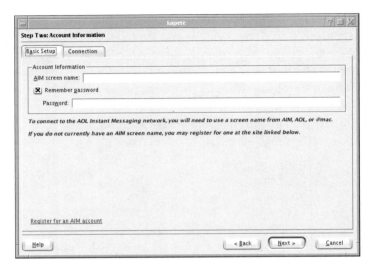

If that's what you want, click the "Connect automatically at startup" box. If not—or if you decide you no longer want automatic startup that you originally set that way, click on that little box to uncheck it.

Introducing IRC

Fewer than one million of all the people in the world with Internet connections use IRC, yet it is one of the most efficient ways there is to organize group or individual chats. IRC is in many ways like an underground "elite" section of the Internet. Most IRC networks are run by volunteers, and while some networks have chat channels for every topic in the world—literally everything from cross-cultural dating to discussions about TV "reality" shows—many of us use it primarily as a rapid way to give and get technical help. This book's author tends to "hang out" on irc.oftc.net and irc.slashnet.org. Another popular network for Linux people is irc.freenode.net, which is where the official #mepis help channel is located.

If you've never used IRC, this is as good a time as any to try it out.

IRC with Kopete

IRC setup is a little more complicated, but not much. You start with the same "Account Wizard" screen. Form there you click "New," then "Next," then "IRC" from the list of messaging services. Another "Next" takes you to the IRC setup screen.

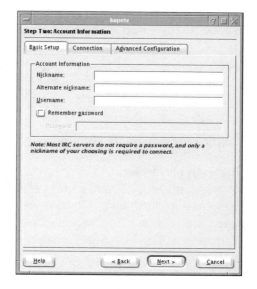

Note that there are three tabs here. You'll need to use at least two of them to get your IRC connection going. Indeed, the one you'll need to use beyond the "Basic Setup" screen where you type in your nickname and username is the "Connection" screen, where you'll type in the IRC server to which you want to connect. While you're on that screen, decide whether or not you want to connect to that network every time you start Kopete.

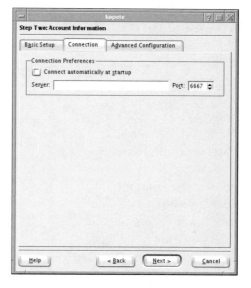

The third IRC setup screen says it's for "Advanced Configuration," but it's not really advanced. You use this screen to set up any channels you want to join automatically, using the standard IRC "/join #channel" command, plus you use it to decide if you want to set up for CCCP file-passing via IRC. (If you're not a skilled IRC user and don't understand all of this, don't worry. You don't need to use IRC at all, and even if you want to *start* using it, all you need to know is which servers and channels you want to join.)

"Which IRC Channels Should I Join?"

The only sane answer to this question is another question: "What are your interests?" There are tens of thousands of IRC channels. Some are centered on computers and software; almost every program included on your *SimplyMepis* CD has at least one dedicated IRC channel where you can go for help, and you can find IRC channels for almost any non-computer interest, from dating to sailing to your favorite video game or TV show.

An obvious first channel for you to join is #mepis on irc.freenode.net. It's the MEPIS help channel. Another one you may want to check for general Linux help, also on irc.freenode.net, is #linux.

To find more channels, a great place to start is the web site SearchIRC.com. It doesn't list every IRC chat room in the world—IRC channels come and go so fast that no one can keep up with the constant changes—but it lists thousands of the more popular ones and even has a little IRC utility built into the Web site you can use to check out a channel before you decide to add it to your Kopete list.

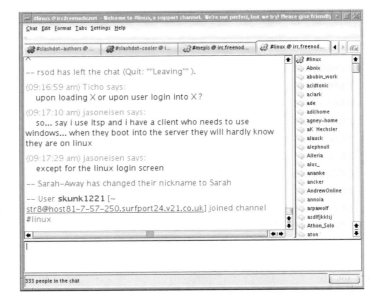

Configuring Kopete's "Look and Feel"

This is not hard, and it's strictly optional. Select the "Settings" option from the top of your Kopete screen, then "Configure Kopete," and from the screen that gives you, either select "Appearance" or Behavior." Either one will give you several tabs to choose, like "General" or "Chat Window." These are areas where experimenting is safe, and even encouraged. At the worst, if you make something look strange, you can go back to the screen

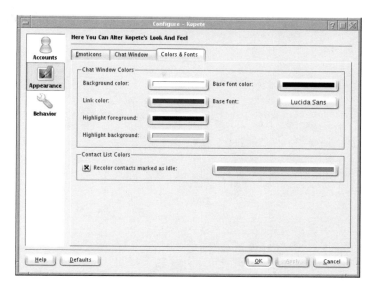

where you made the change and hit the "Defaults" button at the bottom, and everything will go back to the way it was before you started experimenting.

Where to Get Kopete Help

```
LinuxQuestions.org
kopete.kde.org
irc.kde.org, #kopete
```

Chapter 18

gFTP—An Easy, Powerful FTP Program

Y ou can do basic data downloads directly through your Mozilla browser, but when it comes to heavy-duty uploading and downloading, especially to an FTP (File Transfer Protocol) server you manage yourself, nothing beats having a dedicated FTP program. We like gFTP so much that we used it to transfer all *Point & Click Linux!* video, text, and image files. It is the best, most reliable, and most versatile "point and click" FTP program we have ever used.

> ### Read this chapter only if you use FTP
>
> This chapter is intended for experienced FTP users. If you don't use FTP, feel free to skip it. If you want to learn about FTP, your ISP probably has an FTP tutorial online. If not, the one at `www.ftpplanet.com/ftpresources/basics.htm` is fairly good, and if you key the words "FTP tutorial" into any search engine you will find many more.

FTP Has Gotten Easier to Use Over the Last Decade

For many years, basic FTP programs were 100% command line-based. You typed in long strings of text that were only partially in human-readable language to accomplish your goals. People who used command line FTP programs tended to mutter things like "chmod 644 permissions changed user read-only" in their sleep, because if they didn't remember all the commands they couldn't do their jobs. Luckily, command-line FTP is now strictly the province of hard-core Unix and Linux gurus, and the rest of us can get exactly the same results without using a command line or memorizing all those lines of computerese.

gFTP follows the same basic "Local computer files on the left, remote computer files on the right" format as almost every other GUI FTP program. Here's an example of the file structure for the MEPIS.org private "beta test" download server:

We've made that window wider by grabbing the line to its left (just to the right of the "Arrow" buttons) with our mouse and pulling it left until we could see all the information we wanted. All gFTP windows can be resized this easily.

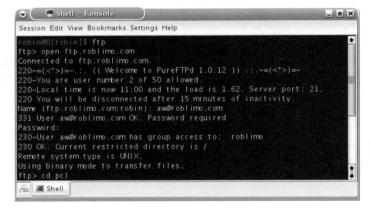

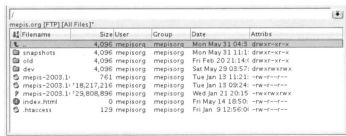

To download (or upload) a file, highlight it with your left mouse button, make sure you're in the correct directory on the computer to which you want to transfer it, and press the appropriate arrow button. Then, if it's a big file that's going to take a long time to transfer, go do something else. gFTP will work fine without you watching. Your gFTP screen will look something like this while the file transfer is in progress:

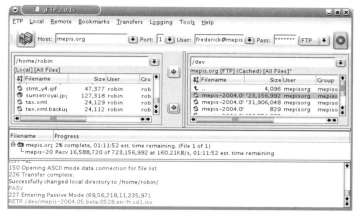

Working with a Remote Server

Log in exactly the same way as in any other FTP client. You can see the form spaces for server name, username, and password in the screenshots. Use them appropriately. You can also add the FTP site you're on as a bookmark so you don't need to enter that information again. Check the "Remember Password" box and even your password will be remembered. Quite a time-saver!

You can either type in remote server directories as filenames in the space above the "file listing" window on the right half of your gFTP screen or navigate the remote server's file system by clicking on directories, folders, and files. After you've found the file or directory you want to transfer or modify, highlight it by clicking on it. To *modify* that file's permissions and characteristics (assuming you have permission to do this on that remote server), right-click on it and choose from the list of commands that will pop up. All your old favorites are there.

Because Linux is simi-
lar to Unix, and all
FTP file commands

are Unix-based, you can make all the same changes on your local files with gFTP, too. This is usually pointless because you have an efficient, built-in file browser that makes file management on your computer easier than doing it through an FTP program. However, it's a cute little trick you can use if, for instance, you spot a typo in a file name while working with FTP and want to change it before you forget.

The gFTP Toolbar

The icon button on the left is what you click to make a connection after you have the correct information (server name, user name, and so on) typed in. Over to the right, the little button that says "FTP" allows you to switch protocols; you can use gFTP for HTTP transfers and—more useful—for secure transfers with SSH (Secure Shell protocol).

The rest of the toolbar functions are self-explanatory. Click on the text menu items at the top of the gFTP window and you'll instantly see what functions are available though each one. Only the "Help" button is disappointing; there is no built-in manual for gFTP. On the other hand, you could argue that there is no need for one since gFTP is so simple, obvious, and stable.

gFTP help and information is available at www.gftp.org.

Chapter 19

K3b—Easy CD Burning Program

We chose K3b as the CD and DVD burning program to include in the *SimplyMEPIS* CD and this book because it is one of the finest and most versatile programs of this type we have ever used, in any operating system. K3b handles music, video, and data equally well, and has no trouble burning the "ISO" (complete file system image) CDs needed to boot your computer directly from its CD drive. This is the program that was used to create the original master version of the *SimplyMEPIS* bootable CD and the video instruction DVD included with this book.

You can also use K3b to copy almost any kind of CD or DVD that doesn't have some sort of built-in copy protection, although you will want to make sure you don't make illegal copies of movies or songs that are protected by copyright laws where you live.

Remember, too, that if your drive won't burn DVDs, no software—not even K3b—can make it into a DVD-burner. Most R/W (Read/Write) drives that can *read* DVDs can't *make* them, even if they do a fine job of writing CDs.

Running K3b

So far we haven't encountered a CD or DVD drive that K3b failed to detect or that needed any setup action beyond clicking "Okay" on the defaults. When you start K3b for the first time it will detect your CD R/W (or DVD R/W) drive and that will be that. You will soon be taken to an opening screen that has a big "Tooltip"' window splashed across it.

As with all other Linux programs, you can keep the
"Tips" windows from show-
ing up when you start the
program by unchecking the
"Show tips on startup" box.
It's probably a good idea to
let them come up at least
the first few times you open
the program—and to act-
ually read them, because
they contain useful information. Or you may want to
click "Next" on the K3b
tooltip window four or five

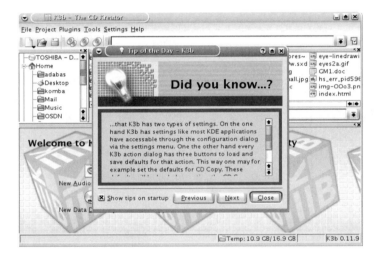

times and read all the tips at one time, then shut them off for the future. (K3b is so easy to use that there aren't a lot of tips, so this might be best.)

Now we have K3b set up (automatically) and ready to run. So let's do something

with it. The main startup screen gives us several choices. We're going to choose "New Data CD Project" because we often create Data CDs. In this case, the data will be a bunch of pictures we took of a sailboat race. We're going to make a CD with all the pictures on it that we can give to the editor of the Sarasota Sailing Squadron's monthly newsletter, "The Burgee," for publication in the next edition.

We have four types of projects from which to choose:

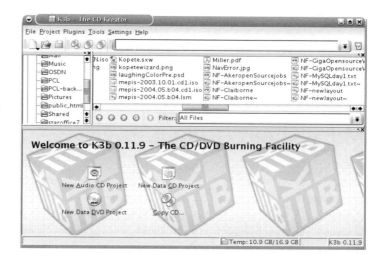

1. New Audio CD Project
2. New Data CD Project
3. New Data DVD Project
4. Copy CD

K3b considers everything other than music "Data," and we're writing to a CD, so we'll choose "New Data CD Project."

After we make that choice, we need to choose the data we want to put on the CD. The top half of our K3b screen is divided into two sections: files on the right, folders on the left. We're going to put an entire "Pictures" folder on CD, so we put our cursor on the "Pictures" directory listing and, while holding our left mouse button, drag it down into the "Current Projects" area, then release the mouse button.

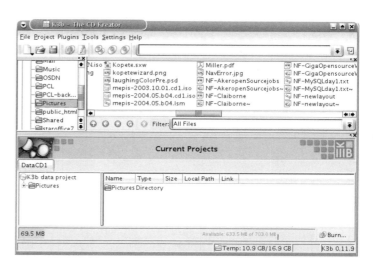

145

We look down in the lower left corner of the window and see that we have 69.4 megabytes of data in our "Pictures" folder, which will easily fit on a single CD. There's only one thing left to do, assuming we've put either a blank recordable CD or a rewritable CD in our drive: Click the "Burn" button in the lower right corner of the K3b window and sit back.

Making a music CD is exactly the same, except you choose "Audio CD Project," and instead of selecting a whole folder at once to put on the CD, you might want to place each file (that is, each piece of music) individually on it so you can set the order in which they'll play on the finished CD. To move files around within the "Project" listing, you just "drag" them to where you want them with the mouse while holding the left mouse button and release the button where you decide they best fit in your custom-made playlist.

More About Using K3b

When using Reusable (Rewritable) CDs, K3b will automatically "blank" them—that is, remove what you had on them before—but will ask you to confirm this action first so you don't delete important material by mistake.

Copying CDs is self-explanatory; just step through the processes as they come up, following the onscreen instructions.

Making or copying DVDs is the same as working with CDs, except you must have a DVD burner and not just a CD burner to use this feature.

Burning ISO images from which your computer can boot directly (like the *SimplyMEPIS* CD in this book) requires a slightly different procedure. Select "Tools," then "CD," then "Burn CD Image." (Or if you have a DVD-write drive, you can burn a bootable DVD instead by clicking "DVD" instead of "CD." After that, select the ISO image you want to put on CD or DVD, and you will get a special screen for ISO burning.)

The built-in K3b "Help" file is surprisingly good. It contains most of the information you'll ever need for daily K3b use. We suggest playing with a rewritable CD for your first experiments, because no matter how good your burning software may be (and K3b is very good indeed) a single wrong move, especially when burning a bootable CD, can leave you with a useless plastic "coaster" instead of correctly stored data. Even though rewritable CDs cost more than "single write" recordable CDs, it is worth the few extra bucks to have some around for testing—and if you regularly back up your most important data on CD (as everyone should but few do), you

can reuse a single rewritable CD over and over for your most current information instead of accumulating a stack of CDs with old data on them.

K3b Information and Help

www.k3b.org
www.MEPIS.org/forum

Chapter 20

The GIMP—A Full-featured Graphics Application

If you're coming from Windows you're probably used to a decent low-end image manipulation program like Paint Shop Pro, CorelDRAW Essentials, or, if you're lucky, a high-end graphics program like Adobe Photoshop. At their most basic level, these applications can digitize and modify photographs or create and edit drawings. At their most powerful, a trained, highly skilled, and experienced user can create amazing works of art with them. But as of this writing none of these programs is available for Linux.

Enter the *GNU Image Manipulation Program*, or the GIMP for short. It's a lightweight but powerful graphics program with an unfortunately awkward interface.

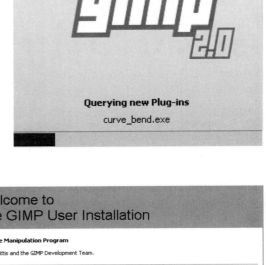

Getting Started

You'll find the GIMP in the Graphics section of your KDE menu. Click on the K-Gear icon in the lower left corner of the screen, then Graphics, then the GIMP.

The first thing you'll see is an orange setup screen.

This screen is simply a welcome message introducing you to the GIMP. You can read it if you like, but there isn't any really valuable information there. Click the "Continue" button. The next screen asks you where you'd like to put the folder that will store your program settings and preferences; it's best just to leave it at the default location, so click on

"Continue." Next, you'll be shown an installation log—you can read it if you like, but it's not necessary. Click "Continue" again and you'll be brought to a screen labeled "Performance Tuning."

If you have a newer computer with a lot of memory (512MB or more) and you'll be working with larger pictures, you may want to increase the tile cache from 64 to 128. This will allow more memory for working with graphics files, but it will not affect your system when you're not using the GIMP. Click "Continue" and you'll find yourself at the Monitor Resolution screen. Leave this

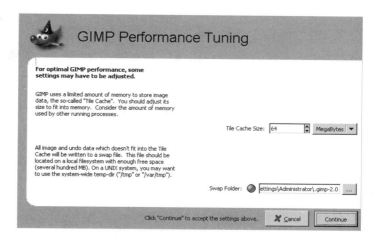

setting at the default; it will use the resolution for which your system is already set. Click "Continue" one last time and you're finished—the program will now start normally.

Using the GIMP

When the program is completely loaded and started, a series of small windows appears on your screen, each containing different tools and functions related to the program. The topmost window will be the GIMP "Tip of the Day," and it'll tell you a different fact about the program every time you start. You can also scroll through the different tips by clicking on the "Next Tip" and "Previous Tip" buttons.

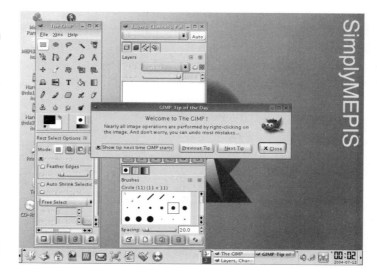

The main GIMP window is labeled the GIMP and it contains the drawing and painting tools that you're used to using in most graphics programs. If the meaning of an icon is not obvious, move

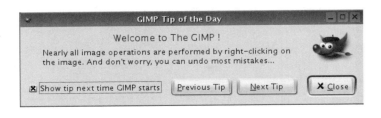

your mouse over the tool icon and a text box will pop up to tell you what it does. The lower portion of the GIMP window is for specific tool options; click on a tool and the lower section changes to show you the ways you can change and modify that tool.

The other window on the screen is titled "Layers, Channels, Paths," and it is primarily for advanced users who deal with layered images. The bottom portion of this window has your brush sizes and shapes, which you'll also have access to in the main GIMP window through a drop-down dialog box. You can safely close the "Layers, Channels, Paths" window if you aren't going to use any of its functions, and if you need any of them later you can bring this window back by choosing "Dialogs" from the File menu, then clicking on "Create New Dock," then selecting "Layers, Channels, Paths." If you do this, you'll notice that your brush selection is gone and the window is smaller than before. If you'd like to get the panel to look exactly the way it was before, it'll require a little customization work. That's no big deal; you can customize almost everything about the GIMP by choosing "File" and selecting "Preferences" from the drop-down menu.

If you move the mouse around the GIMP window you'll notice that it turns into a hand cursor when you move over the center of the menu where the arrow and X icons are. By clicking and dragging this area of the window, you can drag it into its own window or to another part of the main GIMP window. You can also create your own custom window by exploring the Dialogs portion of the File menu.

If you get to a point where you've messed up your GIMP windows and can't get them back, exit the program and delete the .gimp2 entry in your user's home directory by using the Konqueror file manager. It's hidden, so you'll have to select the Show Hidden Files option in your view menu.

After the file is deleted, start up the GIMP again and you'll be back to default settings.

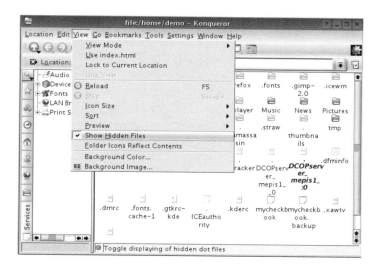

Working with Pictures

To retrieve a pre-existing image file, click on File, then Open, then navigate to the file and click on OK. Another window will open up with the picture in the middle, rulers at the sides, and a menu at the top.

To change the whole picture's properties, such as size, resolution, color depth, or to add special effects or filters, use the menu in the picture window. The main GIMP window's menu is only useful for program functions not related to the picture you're currently working on. You can, of course, use all the available tools in the main GIMP window to alter or manipulate the picture or pictures you're working on.

Scanning and Editing Photos

The GIMP can't scan pictures directly, but it does have the ability to use an external extension to communicate with your scanner. *SimplyMEPIS* comes with both Kooka and xscanimage. Kooka is generally used as a standalone application, but you can call xscanimage from within the GIMP by opening up your File menu, clicking on Acquire, then on xscanimage. The scanning program will open, and you can select your quality and size settings and scan from there.

If you're interested in screen shots, there is another option in the Acquire submenu specifically for that purpose.

Editing photos is fairly simple; you can draw on a photo by selecting the drawing and painting tools in the main GIMP window. You can also add text, crop, or skew and rotate the image, all through the same set of tools. If you want to add special effects, explore the Filters and Script-Fu menus in the image window.

All functions relating directly to the image (including saving and exporting the image) are done through the image window's menus. You can either select them at the top of the window as usual, or you can right-click the image and access all the same menus in a popup dialog box..

Where to Get GIMP Help

The best form of help you can get for the GIMP is online. You can find tutorials to help you learn how to perform specific tasks or to simply learn how to use the GIMP more effectively at this address: `http://www.gimp.org/tutorials/`

The GIMP mailing lists can provide help for more specific problems with the program or its use, but please first read the section on list etiquette: `http://www.gimp.org/mail_lists.html`

Lastly, documentation for the GIMP can be found at this address: `http://wiki.gimp.org/gimp/GimpDocs`

Chapter 21

Digikam—Importing and Organizing Digital Photos

Digikam is a simple digital photo management application. When imported from your camera, your photos can be placed in albums that are automatically sorted chronologically. An easy-to-use interface allows you to connect your camera to your PC so you can transfer your images to your computer in only a few seconds, then—at your command—clear your camera's memory.

Digikam Setup

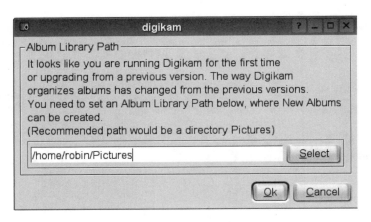

The first screen you see when you start Digikam asks you where you want to store your photos. *SimplyMEPIS* already has a "Pictures" folder, so that's a logical place to put them unless you want to make your own folder under a different name. (Because you can easily move your photos from folder to folder later with the KDE file manager, we'll just put them in "Pictures" for this demonstration.)

Next—and this is purely optional—we can choose how large we want our thumbnails (the miniature "preview" versions of our photos that show on our gallery pages) to be, and at the same time we have a chance to create "Album Collection Types" either by choosing one or more from a built-in list or by clicking "Add" to create a folder with a name you select.

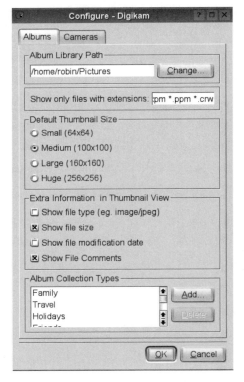

Selecting a Camera

The next step is to hook up a digital camera and set Digikam to work with it. To get to the camera setup utility from the window where we just set up our albums, we click the "Cameras" tab at the top. We also need to have our camera turned on and connected to our computer, usually through our USB port. Now we click "Auto-Detect." The camera we have connected adds itself automatically to our camera inventory without fussing with driver CDs or any of that mess. If you have two digital cameras, hook up the second one, click "Auto-Detect" again, and it, too, will be added to the list. If you have three cameras, or four, or eight, just keep going.

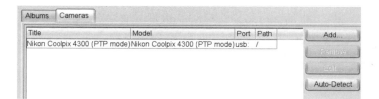

Don't forget to set your camera correctly

The Nikon Coolpix 4300 we used for this demonstration has more than one picture transfer mode. The one Digikam (and most other PC camera programs) uses is called "PTP" (Picture Transfer Protocol), and if your camera isn't set to use the right protocol, you won't be able to transfer pictures. If you have problems uploading photos, the first thing you should check is your camera's settings, not your computer's.

Downloading Pictures

We download pictures by selecting "Cameras" from the top menu line in the main Digikam program window, then using the drop-down menu that gives us to select the camera we currently have connected to our computer.

This gives us thumbnail views of all pictures in our camera's memory.

Album Image Select View Camera Tools Settings Help

We can click on any one of the thumbnails to view it full-size.

Okay, that picture looks decent. In fact, all of them look good enough to keep, so we'll go back to the little filmstrip-like thumbnail view window, and click on the third icon from the left (which pops up a little box that says "download" when we run our cursor over it) to download all four pictures in our camera's memory to our computer.

We have one gallery set up, called "More Pictures," so that's where these photos

will go. If we had more than one gallery, we'd make a choice in the "Download To Album:" line at the bottom of the window or use the "Add Gallery" button to create a new gallery.

Now, if we return to the main Digikam program window and click on our album's name, we have the downloaded pictures in front of us.

We can move pictures from one album to another or reorder them within their original gallery with the usual KDE "drag and drop" actions. We can click on pictures and see them full-sized, use icons to "zoom in" and "zoom out" and there's an icon to the right of the two magnifying glass "zoom" icons we can click to expand the Digikam window to fill our entire

screen—and click again while in full-screen mode to shrink the Digikam window back to normal size.

Altering Photos with Digikam

Double-click on a picture in a Digikam gallery and it shows up full-sized in a new screen.

We can now perform a few simple alterations on it either by right-clicking anywhere on the picture or by using the icons in the top menu to the right of the "full screen" one.

From left to right, these icons let you

- Change the photo's contrast, color and gamma (brightness)

- Rotate it 90, 180 or 270 degrees

- Crop it to eliminate unwanted portions

- Save it after you've made changes

- Undo your changes if you decide you don't like them

As usual, running your cursor over these icons brings up a text box for each one that tells you what it does.

Here's what the photo we used in our "full-sized picture" example (above) looks like when cropped down to show just the part we decided was most important:

Where to Get Digikam Help

When Digikam was chosen for inclusion in *SimplyMEPIS* it was a new program, still in beta but fully functional. If you update your *SimplyMEPIS* install by using the free MEPIS subscription offer on this book's last page, you will get a new, more stable version of Digikam. You can keep track of Digikam updates and find the latest Digikam documentation at `digikam.sourceforge.net`—and you'll find that the "Help" button at the top of every Digikam screen opens a complete and readable Digikam manual.

Chapter 22

Games!— Amusements Included with the *SimplyMEPIS* CD

MEPIS Linux isn't all business. It has a number of built-in games and toys that will help keep your head clear for more serious endeavors. Later you can download more Linux games, but there are more than enough on the CD to get you going—so many that we aren't going to highlight them all here but will stick to a few of the most popular ones.

These games take no setup to run. You can start playing them as soon as you boot your computer from the *SimplyMEPIS* CD. One warning, though: This book's author and the creators of MEPIS, Debian, KDE, the individual games, and Linux itself are *not* responsible for loss of productive time (or valuable Linux learning time) due to excessive use of addictive games and other toys....

Card Games

Patience (Solitaire)

This is your basic solitaire game. Reach it by clicking on your "K-Gear" icon, choosing "Games," then "Card Games," then "Patience."

You can now play as long as you like. Or you can spend a few moments customizing the cards' appearance by clicking "Settings," then "Switch Cards." From "Settings" you'll also see a "Game Type" choice that gives you 18 different one-player patience-type card games. If you run into one that's unfamiliar to you, but still want to give it a try, the "Game" top menu choice has a "Demo" feature you

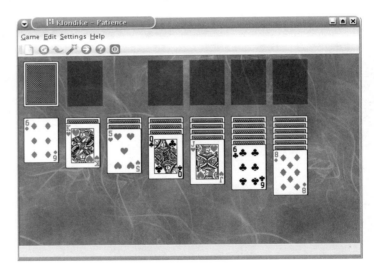

can click to see how the game is played. While you're learning a new game, you can click on the wand icon at the top to get a hint or two.

If that isn't enough help, you can click "Help" and see the rules for each "Patience" game.

KPoker

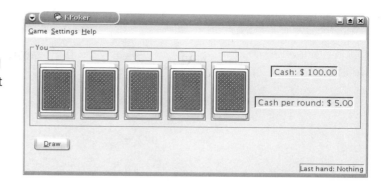

It's five-card draw. "Settings" gives you several choices, including card front and back design and other options. "Game" takes you to three choices. You can "Quit" or "Save" (this game) if your boss catches you playing when you shouldn't be. Or you can choose "New Game" and even make it a two-person game, with your computer on the other side of the virtual poker table.

And if you think playing against "Computer 1" doesn't sound quite as snappy as playing against "Cochise Charlie" or "Bisbee Bill," go ahead and make that change. You can change your name, too, if you like. You can adjust the amount of money you all bring to the table if you want to play for higher (or lower) stakes than the default $100. But that's about all the changes you can make in KPoker.

Arcade Games

Frozen Bubble

Frozen Bubble is a simple looking amusement with dopey arcade game background music, but writing a book chapter on it can take hours of research. That research might *look* like the author is just screwing around and playing a game, but this is an illusion. Writing a book like *Point & Click Linux!* means thoroughly testing every program mentioned, including getting to level 47 in Frozen Bubble.

A few notes about Frozen Bubble:

- Your mouse doesn't work in Frozen Bubble. You scroll through the list of choices you see when you first start it up with your "arrow" keys and make selections with your shift bar.
- When you play the game, the arrow keys are your controls.
- Bank Shots are important, and the most obvious shot is not always the best one.
- Watch the next ball up, not just the one you're about to shoot.

This is a scarily addictive game for some people. Be careful not to let it take up too much of your time.

Tux Racer

Tux the Penguin slides down a slalom-type course as fast as he can, gobbling herring as he goes. Sometimes he screws up and goes off course. He uses his flippers to speed up and digs his feet into the snow to slow down.

The faster Tux goes, and the more herring he grabs, the higher his score. One or two can play.

Note: This game will work properly *only* if you have a 3-D Video card and MEPIS Linux has detected it correctly. If you start Tux Racer and it looks awful, you do not have the correct video setup. For advice, check `www.mepis.org/forum`.

TuxKart

It's a go-kart racing game, once again starring the Linux mascot, Tux the Penguin. The graphics aren't as smooth as Tuxracer's, but there are six racetracks, only one of which resembles a traditional racetrack. It's a simple "go fast" game, but it has enough wrinkles and tricks that you might want to glance at its home site, `tuxkart.source-forge.net`, at some point.

Note: Like TuxRacer, TuxKart needs 3D Video.

Board Games

Backgammon

If you know how to play Backgammon, this program's behavior is obvious. If not, the "Help" button will give you a rough idea of how the game is played, but you'd be better off consulting a book that will really teach it to you.

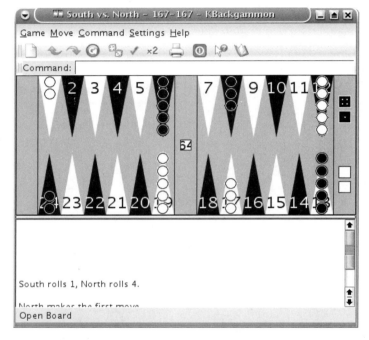

Chess

The *SimplyMEPIS* CD contains only a basic chessboard. You'll need to supply your own two players. There's an excellent free GNUChess program available that will allow you to play against your computer, but it was too big to fit on a single CD along with all the other software we included. After you get a little practice with Linux it will be no trouble to download and install on your own.

KMahjongg

A classic Chinese board game played with tiles whose distinctive clack-clack combines with players' chatter to give it a distinct sound.

The KMahjongg board included with the KDE desktop that's part of MEPISLinux is technically accurate, but leaves out the clack-clack tile sounds, which some Mah Jongg enthusiasts will find disheartening, although others will probably find it a welcome relief.

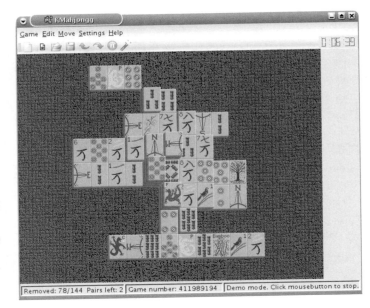

Tactics and Strategy

Klickety is a "remove as many tiles from the board as you can in the shortest possible time" board game, a fine way to while away the hours instead of working—or as we writers like to say, "while waiting for inspiration to strike." It's depressing when the best score you get yourself is 12, and you check online records and see that many players consistently get "0" scores, which is as high (low) as you can go in Klickety. More practice is obviously needed!

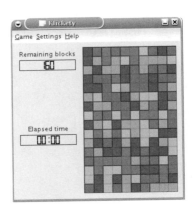

KBattleship is a KDE/Linux variant of the classic "Battleship" naval maneuvering game. You can play against your computer or, by accessing the Handbook through the "Help" button, learn how to play against others either through a local computer network or over the Internet.

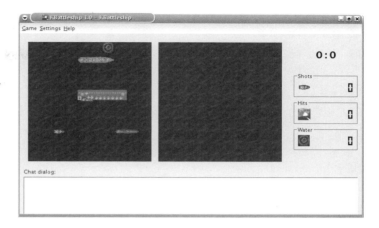

Other Games for Linux

Check "Potato Guy" in the "Kidsgames" category. It's a party hoot for adults, too, although it's best in the hands of a four-year-old who enjoys making funny faces. For older youngsters, check the "Edutainment" category for games that teach as you play them, including a typing tutor suitable not only for beginners but also for experienced typists who want to brush up on their skills or increase their speed and accuracy.

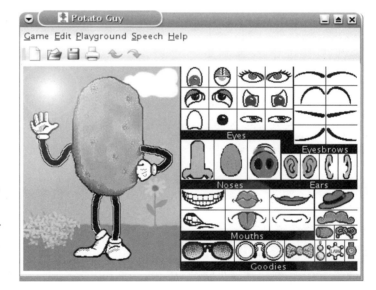

And that's not all! There are at least a dozen other games already installed for your pleasure in various categories, plus thousands more——for all ages—available for free download, ranging from simple text challenges to complex online extravaganzas that take place in their own universes.

We'll show you how to get more games (and give you an idea of what's available) in Chapter 24, "Downloading and Installing Software."

Chapter 23

Other *SimplyMEPIS* Applications

The programs we've described so far are the ones included on the *SimplyMEPIS* CD that we feel are necessary to get you going with Linux right away. There are dozens of others there, too, that can do many things. This is a brief list of them, broken down by menu category (Editors, Internet, System, and so on). These are all preinstalled on your computer automatically; all you need to do to use them is click on their names in the menu listings that appear when you click the "K-Gear" icon in the lower left hand corner of your screen. (If you end up using any of these programs often, you can add them to your bottom-of-the-screen control panel; we'll learn how to do that in Chapter 26, "Customizing Linux.")

We'll start with the "Editors" category.

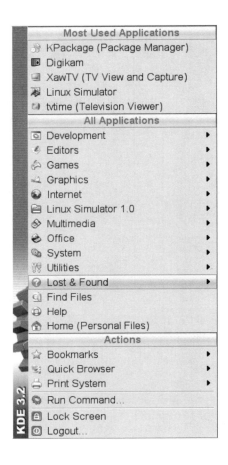

Editors

Bluefish and ***Quanta+*** are both editors designed to help you build professional-level Web sites. They are not for HTML beginners; both assume you have a working knowledge of HTML and possibly CSS (Cascading Style Sheets), Javascript, and

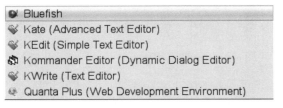

other components of a modern, full-featured Web presence. They are also useful for people who write text that is going to appear on the WWW rather than in print.

Kommander is included because it's really part of **Quanta+** but can also be used as a standalone program if you need to create advanced features on an interactive Web page.

Kate and **KEdit** are text editors similar to **KWrite**, which we have already discussed at length. They're in your menu because some people like one or the other of them more than **KWrite**, the simple KDE text editor preferred by this book's author. This is a matter of personal taste, so we've included these alternatives for you to try. Use whichever one you like; as we keep saying, it's *your* computer, not ours.

Games

We covered the main ones earlier; we're going to leave you to explore the rest of the included ones on your own. In our next section we'll turn you on to some excellent (and popular) ones you may want to download. We would have liked to include them for you, but you can only put so much on one CD…

Graphics

This looks like an incredible number of programs, but most of them in the "More Programs" group sticking out to the right are utilities that are called on by other programs, not programs you're likely to use all by themselves. But many of the programs in the main graphics menu are directly useful on their own. Some highlights:

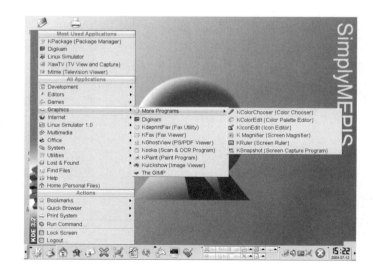

KDEPrintFAX is a fax program that works with several well-known commercial Internet fax services, notably HylaFax (`www.hylafax.org/`) and eFax (`www.efax.com`). It will also work with your modem, assuming it's already set up with the *KPPP* utility, and can even be used to fax OpenOffice.org documents directly from OOo with a little advanced setup work that's beyond the scope of this book. **KFax** is simply a fax viewer that allows you to read faxes sent to you as email attachments or by other means. (Remember, faxes are graphics, not text; you need a graphics application to read them.)

KGhostView is a program that reads documents formatted in Abobe's PDF and PostScript formats. You'll probably use it more through your Web browser than by itself; it's the program your browser automatically calls whenever you click on a PDF document. There's also an Adobe Reader program available from Adobe, the company that created the PDF format, but licensing restrictions

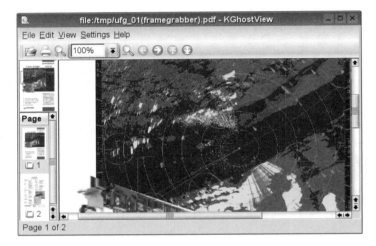

make it hard to include in a free Linux CD that you are allowed (even encouraged) to copy and share with friends and coworkers.

Kooka is a scanner program that works with most common home and small office scanners and can even use OCR (Optical Character Recognition) to turn many scanned documents into computer-editable text files. It has a well-written illustrated manual built into it; click the "Help" button on the main **Kooka** screen to read it.

KPaint is a very basic drawing program. You may want to use it for adding lines and arrows to an existing graphic or to draw simple shapes, but that's probably about it. For more serious graphics work you'll want to use the **GIMP**.

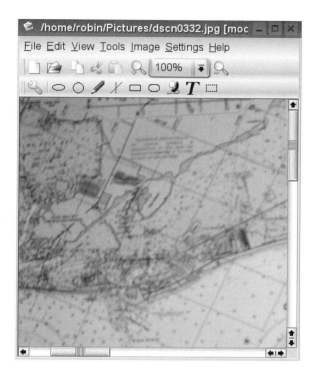

Kwickshow is an image viewer that pops up automatically when you click on a photo or other image file. And last—so last that it's at the bottom of the "More Programs" window in the graphics menu, but far from least—is **KSnapshot**, the versatile screenshot program that was used to capture almost every image in this book.

Internet

Again, there is a mighty number of programs. We've covered the **Mozilla** Web browser and email client, and under "Connection" (one of the sub-menus) we've discussed **KPPP**, the dialup utility, and **ADSL/PPoE** for old-style DSL connections. The only "Connections" we haven't covered are the **KWifiWiManager**, which is only useful if you have a wireless LAN connection (and is pretty self-explanatory after you've set up a wireless network), and **Smb4K**, a Samba utility that lets us share files with Windows computers on our LAN (Local Area Network) that we'll cover a little later on, in the "Beyond the Basics" section.

There are only four applications In the Internet menu's "More Programs" submenu.

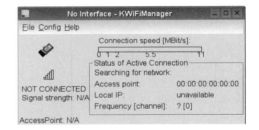

Camstream is a utility program for streaming Webcams through a video input card. **KPPP Log Viewer** monitors modem use. It's useful primarily for people who pay for dialup Internet connections by the minute or have limits on the number of hours they can use their connections each month without paying extra. **KStreamRipper** records streaming audio to your hard disk. **Remote Desktop Connection** is a VNC (Virtual Network Computer) utility that lets you use your Linux computer to remotely control other computers. (If you have never done this before, you'll want to read this program's "Help" file and perhaps learn a little bit about VNC in general before trying to set up a VNC connection between two computers.)

The rest of the important Internet applications are in the main "Internet" menu. **KMail** is an email program many Linux users prefer to Mozilla, and many use **Konqueror** not only for file management but also as their Web browser. **Pan** is a well-regarded newsgroup reader for those who still enjoy Usenet. **Skype** is a new Internet telephony service; it's free to use from computer to computer, but it costs a small amount to call from your computer to a regular telephone. And **Straw** is a new program that can bring RSS headline feeds from all your favorite news sites and blogs to your desktop with no programming knowledge. (It's amazingly easy to set up.)

Multimedia

Again, a mighty-looking selection—and yet again, several of these programs are usually called up automatically, in this case by your Web browser. These programs include **RealPlayer 8**, **KMplayer**, **XMMS**, and **Xine**, all of which open specific types of multimedia files as you download them. But **XMMS** can also be used on its own to play audio from CDs, as can **KsCD**. You'll

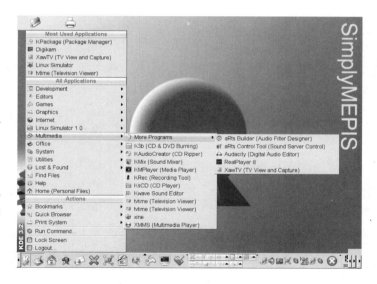

want to try both of these and decide which one you like best. (Hint: **XMMS** looks pretty blah, but it has many great built-in features.)

KAudioCreator takes music from your CDs and saves it to your hard drive. **KMix** is the sound mixer you bring up when you click the little loudspeaker icon on your control panel. **KRec** is a surprisingly sophisticated program (especially consider-

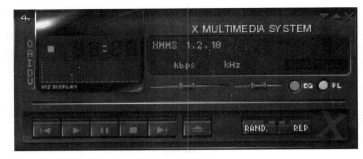

ing the price) that works with **KMix** and the **aRts** control tool to help you create and edit your own voice and music files from your computer's microphone input and other audio sources you choose.

We've already gone over **K3B**; **KWave** is a sound editing program more oriented toward working with exist-
ing audio files than KRec. You might want to use it to create little snippets of music or your own DJ-style "mixes."

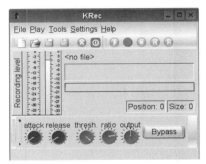

And at the bottom of the "More Programs" menu we find another hidden gem: **XawTV**. If you have a WinTV or other popular TV tuner card, **XawTV** will not only let you watch TV on your PC monitor, but can record shows for you so you can watch them later. Very nice!

Kwave
A sound editor for KDE

Office

There are only two programs here that we haven't covered already. The first is **Planner**, a very new and still slightly experimental program we feel is well worth a test; by the time you read this there will almost certainly be a new, better version available than what you see in this illustration—which you'll note is of version 0.11, with 1.0 usually being the "ready for prime time" point in a program's development. But we're already impressed with **Planner**, so here it is.

Another gem is **Scribus**, a complete, professional-level desktop publishing program for Linux. If you've priced desktop publishing software lately, after you try **Scribus** you'll realize that it alone is worth the cost of the entire *Point & Click Linux!* package many times over. If you're in a business (or have a hobby) that requires desktop publishing, having **Scribus** available will more than pay back all the time you spend learning how to use Linux. Yes, it's really that good—and new versions come out steadily, each one better than the last.

System

We're starting to move into systems administrator territory here. If you're a sysadmin just moving to Linux, these tools will make your life a lot easier than it would be without them. If you're not a sysadmin, this part of your KDE menu is where you start taking full control of your computer in a way you can't with the most popular proprietary PC operating systems.

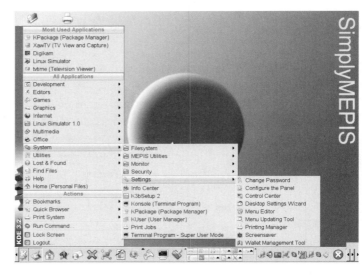

We'll cover most of the **System** tools in this book's "Beyond the Basics" section, which is coming up in just a few pages. Right now, we'll just take a look at a few of the simpler ones.

A good place to start is the KDE **Info Center**. This utility will tell you nearly everything about your PC.

We're looking at our computer's memory use. If you don't understand everything going on here, don't worry. You can click through other characteristics. Some listings will be interesting and some will be puzzling. The more you know about your computer's inner workings, the fewer entries that will be puzzling. But it's all fun to know, even if you don't understand it all at first. (And no, you don't need to know all this stuff to use Linux. The system will

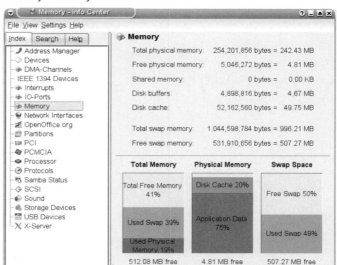

function perfectly well on its own—but if you choose to learn, you may be able to hot-rod your computer a bit by customizing a few settings here and there.)

Another good part of the *System* menu to check out is the *Monitor* submenu.

There are only four listings here. The first one, **KCPULIoad**, tells you how much work your computer CPU (Central Processing Unit) is doing at any given moment. Click on this entry and you'll get a 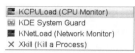 little icon toward the right end of your control panel, kind of like the constantly moving "gas mileage" figure new cars often give you. Click on the icon and you get a little box that gives you those figures as text. Fun! (And useful; if your computer is working so hard that you're seeing 80% CPU usage or higher, you may want to consider running fewer programs at once to keep your computer from slowing down.)

The second listing here is the **KDE System Guard**. This is a powerful tool for systems administrators, and is good to know about even if you consider yourself an ordinary desktop computer user with no real desire to become a Linux wizard. A few minutes pok- 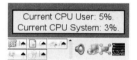 ing around the **KDE System Guard** Handbook (click the inevitable "Help" button to bring it up) can teach you a lot about how computers and networks operate. So can looking at the various **KDE System Guard** functions. Again, you may not understand everything you see here. But even if you don't, it's nice to take a little peek at what's going on under the hood, as it were.

KNetLoad tells you about your network and how it's working, such as how fast, and how much data you're transferring. If the numbers drop to zero, your connection is broken. And even if it's just slower than usual, you may want to do something about it, even if that "something" is calling your ISP to ask what's going on. (At least you *know* there's a problem instead of guessing.)

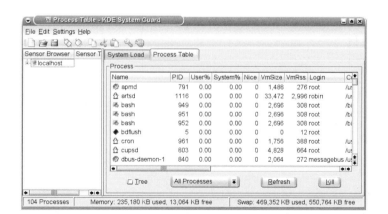

KNetLoad is another icon that gives you text statistics when you click on it.

XKill is a last-ditch thing. Click on **XKill**, then click on a program window that's frozen up or otherwise not behaving right, and **POOF!** that program shuts down and disappears. The only program that may

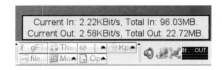

give you trouble after being killed this way (which, thankfully, it almost never needs) is Mozilla. If you **XKill** Mozilla, you may need to reboot your PC to get Mozilla working correctly again.

Utilities

These are small programs that do this and that. We'll cover **Ark**, the archiving tool, in the next chapter. The other utilities are self-explanatory. Just click on them and see what happens. Not everybody finds all these little programs useful, but enough people find enough of them helpful that they're here for you.

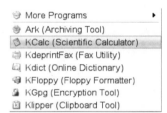

And with that, we'll take a break. After the break, it will be time to start exploring some of the ways you can customize Linux by adding (or removing) software and generally changing things around to suit your personal taste.

Section III

Beyond the Basics

Chapter 24

Downloading and Installing Software

Linux software installation was difficult back in the bad old days. It got easier with the development of the Red Hat Package Management (RPM) system, and even easier with the Debian apt (a package tool) system, because in addition to installing the software you need, apt makes sure any other software your selected program needs to operate is automatically installed along with it. Still, apt is a command-line application that intimidates many computer users, so MEPIS uses a customized version of *KPackage*, a software management program that is part of KDE, to make working with Debian's apt and apt-get utility click-click simple.

The list of programs in the **KPackage** screen shown here is of software programs already installed on your computer. Many of them are background utilities that control basic computer functions you don't need to think about as you sit at your keyboard, the sort of thing all operating systems have buried somewhere

deep inside them but don't let you look at or change. This is one of the great things about open source software like Linux. Nothing is hidden from you. This is also part of its security. There is no way spyware or other software you don't want can be hidden on your computer. Even if you don't spot the evil software yourself, someone else is likely to notice it, and if you check Linux information sites like Linux.com regularly, you can keep up with the latest changes—and easily download and install any security patches with **KPackage**.

Choosing Your Package Sources

This is the first step in setting up to install new software: You need to decide where you're going to get it. This isn't done with **KPackage**, but through the **MEPIS System Center** you reach either by clicking the appropriate desktop icon or selecting it from the "System" section of your main software menu.

When you click that **System Center** icon, the first thing you'll see is a request for your root password.

Why You Need to Type Your Root Password Here

You need to type in your root password almost every time you do anything that can affect your whole computer. This is an inconvenience, but it's a tiny one compared to the damage a single virus could do, not to mention the computer havoc a small child or pet can cause by clicking random keys. It's a worthwhile inconvenience, rather like making sure you lock your door when you leave your house.

So we've spent the second it takes to type in our password and we're at the same **MEPIS System Center** screen we saw when we were setting up our networking—except this time we click on the "Package Management" choice and the right side looks entirely different.

In this illustration, you see you have several software sources you can choose:

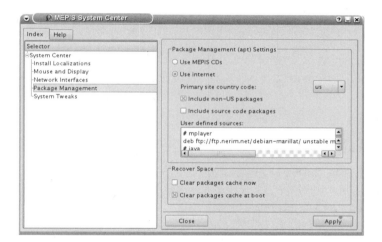

- "Use MEPIS CDs" is for people who have purchased additional software CDs through the MEPIS.org Web site either because they don't have an Internet connection fat or reliable enough for software downloading or because they're willing to pay a nominal fee in return for the convenience of getting their software on CDs.

- "Use Internet" connects you to the Debian server pool that's chock-full of excellent free software. (Learn more about Debian in Chapter 28, "Joining the Linux Community.")

- "Include non-US packages" connects you to servers that carry software that is usually useful and well written, but may not be legal for U.S. residents to use because of patent or copyright restrictions.

- "User defined sources" have several trusted, private servers listed for special software; you can add more if you like—and if you subscribe to the MEPIS private servers, this is where you paste in your subscription information.

189

The most conservative choice is a MEPIS subscription or purchasing MEPIS CDs. This way, every single program will have been tested and proven to work correctly with other MEPIS software. Slightly riskier, but still quite safe, is the "use Internet" option. It connects you to the volunteer-run Debian servers. Programs on these servers have all been tested, but not necessarily with all other programs available. Note that we are not talking about virus worries or other *major* risks, just that you may download a program and find it doesn't work correctly with MEPIS—and need to click a few times to uninstall it. Next come the "non-US" packages. Remember, these may be programs that are not legal under U.S. law, so if you are in the U.S. you use them strictly at your own risk.

"Include source code packages" is a special case. This is for those of you who are either programmers or learning how to program, and want to examine (and perhaps change) the code behind some of the software on your computer.

But enough of that. For this demonstration we'll "Use Internet," so it's time to click "Apply" and call up **KPackage** by clicking the K-Gear in your control panel and going to the "System" submenu. (At this point you can close the MEPIS System Center. Or you can leave it open. It doesn't matter one way or the other.)

Using KPackage

The first thing we want to do is have **KPackage** check the Debian servers for the latest software updates. We do this by using the "Special" link in the upper left hand corner of the

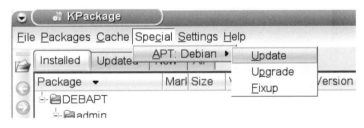

screen to take us to "APT: Debian ->" and from there to "Update," which we click, and then type in our root password when asked.

When we started **KPackage**, it checked our computer to see exactly what programs were installed. Now we're going to wait another few seconds (or longer on a slow Internet connection) while **KPackage** downloads the latest software information for us. (If you see a note that a server or two isn't available, don't worry. There are many Debian "mirror" servers, and if several of them aren't working properly at the moment it doesn't stop us; our apt program automatically finds *working* download servers for us.)

Next, we select the tab "all" so that we have a full list not only of the software we already have installed, but also of the 10,000+ packages available for download.

When that's done, we can select a specific package to download and install. The easiest way to do this if you know the name of the program you want is to use the search tool, which you call up by clicking on the top (of two) magnifying glass icons on the left edge of the *KPackage* window. We're going to search for *Abiword*, a word processing program that doesn't have all of OpenOffice.org's features, but loads much faster and is somewhat easier to use.

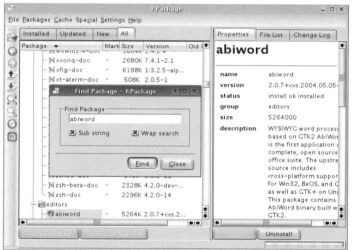

We can read a little about **Abiword** in the right-side KPackage window. And if we want to learn more,

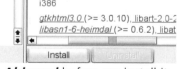

there's a Web site listed where we can go and learn all about **Abiword** before we install it. But that's almost a "Why bother?" thing. Installing (and uninstalling) software with the mighty team of Debian, MEPIS, and KPackage on our side makes it easier to simply download and try it, which we do by clicking the install button below the right-side window.

Getting the Right Software Package

In our search for **Abiword** we also found several related packages. These packages are either **Abiword** add-ons that will be installed automatically with the main package or may be specialty "development" routines useful only for those of you who are programmers and systems administrators who want to modify **Abiword** in some way, but they are not the **Abiword** program itself. Always make sure you get the "plain" package name you are searching for, not something related to it. It's a good idea to get into the habit of checking the right-panel description before downloading to make sure you're getting exactly what you want instead of something that'll make you say, "Huh?!"

Successful installation

When we click that "Install" button we get the "Install" window, which shows not only the program we want to download but also any other programs that will automatically be installed along with it. All we need to do now is click "Install" on this screen to confirm that yes, we really do want to install this program and everything that goes with it, then sit back while things happen.

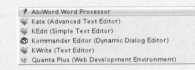

When the install is finished, you'll see a message at the bottom of the install window that says "RESULTS = 0." You may see some messages on the way to this that look like something or other isn't working right, but they are usually the result of one or two Debian servers out of many not working right or being down for maintenance, and you can safely ignore those messages.

The real proof that your installation is successful is that your new program is added to your menus, and we see that **Abiword** is now listed in "Editors," right where it should be.

Uninstalling Software

This is even easier than installing. You can find a program you want to uninstall with the same search tool you used to find one to install, and can cut the search time down by only searching "Installed" software.

The only difference on the main **KPackage** screen, after we find the package we want to uninstall, is that we click "Uninstall" instead of "Install."

On the "Install" screen there is one additional step we want to take before we do our uninstall, namely clicking the "Test (do not uninstall)" checkbox before uninstalling. This will bring up a list of other programs that might be automatically uninstalled too, and will warn us if they might affect other software we want to keep. This kind of problem is very rare, and you can use your *SimplyMEPIS* CD to repair anything you break accidentally, but better safe than sorry, right?

If only the program you want to uninstall shows up, you are safe. Unselect "Test (do not uninstall)" and go to it. The software package you no longer want will quietly disappear without a bit of fuss.

Where to get software installation help:

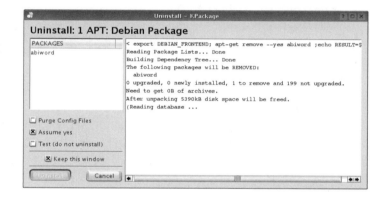

Mepis.org/forum is "the" place to go for answers to KPackage questions.

Other Software You Might Want to Try

Your *SimplyMEPIS* CD only contains a fraction of the software available for Linux. The following is a partial list of additional software available through the MEPIS servers or from MEPIS on CD. It's only a tiny taste of what's there because the complete list would have taken 69 pages and constantly has new software added to it, so you'd need to check the latest version at MEPIS.org anyway.

Beyond that, don't forget, there are another 10,000+ Debian packages waiting for you—a list that would occupy nearly 1,000 pages in a book like this one. Some of your options include:

- **Abiword**—Lightweight, flexible word processor that can read most Microsoft Word files
- **Brahms**—Music editor and MIDI sequencer
- **Cinepaint**—Motion picture image retouching tool
- **Emacs20**—GNU Emacs editor
- **Everybuddy**—All-in-one instant messaging client
- **Evolution**—Groupware suite that effectively replaces Microsoft Outlook (minus the viruses and worms) and can, with the addition of a free connector utility, work with Microsoft Exchange servers
- **Festival**—Multi-lingual speech synthesizer system; makes your typed words talk
- **Flightgear**—Flight simulator program based on sophisticated technology originally developed for the U.S. military
- **Freeciv-client-gtk**—Program needed to join the worldwide Freeciv online multiplayer strategy game (`www.freeciv.org`)
- **Gatos**—All-in-Wonder TV capture software, assuming you have an ATI All-in-Wonder card; software for the more common WinTV and related TV cards is already installed on your system
- **Gnome-desktop-environment**—MEPIS uses the KDE Desktop, but the Gnome Desktop has many devotees; you may want to try it one day
- **Mozilla-Firefox**—Web browser based on Mozilla that almost made it onto the *SimplyMEPIS* CD; by the time you read this, may be better than the original Mozilla
- **Snort**—Network intrusion detection tool that can help you see if bad hackers are trying to get into your computer or network

Just a Few Out of Thousands

These is just a tiny taste of what's available to you beyond the *SimplyMepis* CD. There are endless programs for Linux that you can download and install with a few clicks. One of your best sources for information on them is `www.freshmeat.net`, a Web site that is widely recognized as one of the Web's most comprehensive and up-to-date Linux software lists.

Chapter 25

Cooperating with Windows

There's no denying it: We may use Linux and like it, but there may be programs we need to use that are only available (right now) for Windows, and we must often share computer networks with people who run Windows. Luckily, there are ways we can use Windows software in Linux—even run Windows inside Linux—and network with Windows computers.

CrossOver Office

CrossOver Office is software that runs many Windows applications and plug-ins in Linux. It's a commercial program, but costs much less than a standalone copy of Windows, and after you install it on your computer it only takes a click or two to install a Windows program "inside" it.

When installed, your Windows application will integrate directly with your KDE desktop. Just click and run your application exactly as you would in Windows.

CrossOver Office lets you use many Windows Web browser plug-ins directly with your Linux browser. The most important one is probably the one needed to play Windows Media Player movies and sound. You can play these formats through MPlayer (with the addition of the *w32codecs* you can download and install through KPackage with a few simple clicks) but may not necessarily be legal in the United States due to software patent and copyright laws, whereas CrossOver Office is entirely legal anywhere in the world.

CrossOver Office officially supported these Windows programs in July 2004, with more constantly being added to the list:

- Microsoft Office XP, 2000 and 97
  - Microsoft Word
  - Microsoft Excel
  - Microsoft PowerPoint
  - Microsoft Outlook
  - Microsoft Internet Explorer
- Microsoft Access
- Microsoft Project

- Adobe Photoshop
- Microsoft Visio
- Lotus Notes 5.0 and 6.5.1
- Quicken
- Various Web browser plug-ins
- QuickTime
- Shockwave Director
- Windows Media Player 6.4

There are two versions of CrossOver Office available: one for home use on a single computer, and one that's designed for professional installations on multiple computers. You can purchase a copy of either one through `MEPIS.org` or directly from `CodeWeavers.com`.

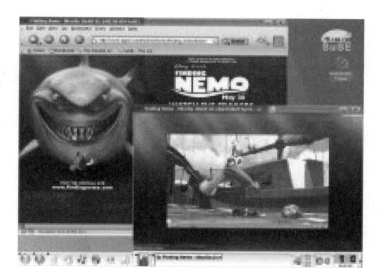

NeTraverse Win4Lin

While CrossOver Office runs *some* Windows applications in Linux, Win4Lin actually runs Windows in Linux, which means virtually all Windows applications work well. One big catch is that in order to use Win4Lin you need to have a copy of Windows around that you can legally load on your Linux computer. The other big Win4Lin catch is that as late as mid-2004 it would still only work with Windows 95, 98, and ME, but you may want to check MEPIS.org to see if this has changed since then. Last we heard while writing this book, a new XP-enabled version of Win4Lin was scheduled for release by the end of 2004.

There are some special Linux kernel modifications needed to run Win4Lin, but they're already built into MEPIS so installation is painless, and installing Windows programs on Windows running on Win4Lin under Linux is faster than installing them in a regular Windows computer because rebooting Windows in Win4Lin is much faster than booting Windows all by itself.

Networking with Windows Machines Using Samba

By Jem Matzan

Even if we don't use any Windows programs ourselves, we may still need to work with Windows computers on a home or office network. We do this with a program called Samba that lets us read Windows files directly from our Linux computer.

Samba: The Server Message Block Client

In order for Linux to access a Windows network, it must use the SMB (Server Message Block) network file-sharing protocol. *SimplyMEPIS* uses a program called Samba to access Windows shares using that protocol.

Unfortunately, the process for using Samba to get Windows to access Linux network shares is much more complicated to set up and configure in both Linux and Windows, so in this chapter we're only going to deal with accessing Windows shares. For this example we're going to assume you have a Windows machine that has already been set up for a workgroup-based network.

The smb4k Utility

In the lower right-hand corner of your screen you'll notice a green and blue icon. That's your Samba client already running, scanning for Windows networks to connect to. Left-click on the icon to bring up the Share Browser.

As you can see, all your Windows workgroups are listed in the left-hand portion of the window. In this example the name of our workgroup is, appropriately, **workgroup**. This is the default name for most versions of Windows; Windows XP's default workgroup name is **mshome**. Aside from defaults, you may have chosen your own workgroup name when you set up your network, or you might have multiple workgroups for different purposes throughout your home or office.

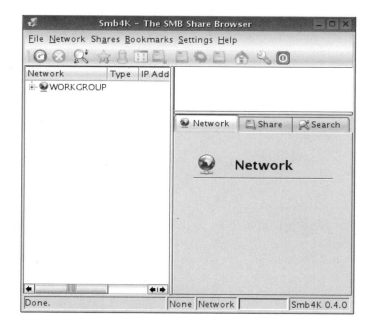

199

Left-click on your workgroup entry to list all the computers currently connected to it. In our example, we only have one computer on the workgroup, and its name is **amd64**. Click on the computer that you would like to access; this brings up the login window.

The login window wants a username and password from you. Enter the name and password of a Windows user on the computer you're

logging into. So if your Windows user's name is **dirkgently** and your password is **iluvdadams**, enter that information in the fields provided. You can always log in as Administrator, but that isn't advised for normal work because the Administrator user has ultimate power on the Windows system, and this poses a security risk. Remember not to use your Linux username and password here; you're logging into a Windows machine remotely, and it doesn't know or care about Linux users.

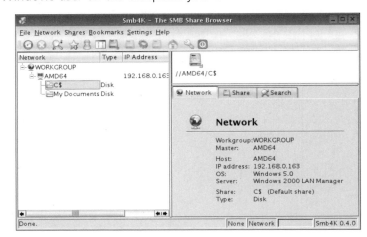

When you're logged into the amd64 machine, you'll be able to see all of its shared directories. In our example we have two shared directories: the root directory and the My Documents folder. When you click on one of these listings, Samba will mount that share in a directory called Smb4k in your user's home directory. It'll also show up in the upper right portion of the Smb4k window. You can mount as many shares as you like.

Alternatively, you can access your mounted shares by right clicking on the Smb4k System Tray icon in the lower right corner of your KDE menu bar. This will bring up a small popup menu. Click on the Mounted Shares option and the menu expands to the right, revealing your currently mounted shares. Click on one of them and a new window with the contents of that share will open.

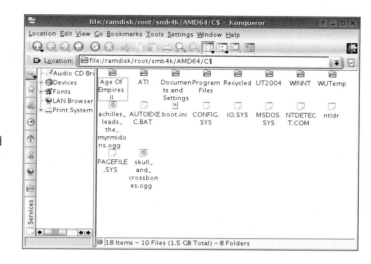

Everything works in this window as it does in a normal Konqueror window. You can drag and drop, rename, copy, move, delete, and create files just as if they were on your local machine.

Configuring the Samba Client

If you right-click on the Smb4k tray icon and bring up the popup dialog again, you'll notice there's an option for Configuring Smb4k. This option can also be found in the SMB Share Browser window in the Settings menu. Click on Configuring Smb4k to see some of the settings and preferences for Smb4k.

The most useful options are probably going to be in the Shares portion of the configuration window. Here you can choose to automatically mount some or all of your network shares when Smb4k starts. Most of the other options are for more advanced users with special network considerations.

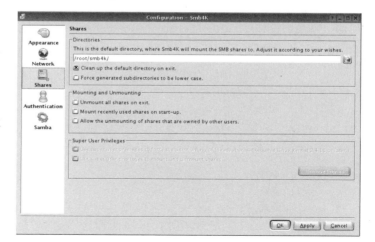

Getting Help with Samba and Smb4k

Samba itself is a fairly broad topic; it might be more useful to look for help related directly to Smb4k instead. Unfortunately, as of this writing, the Smb4k handbook is only an empty placeholder and contains no information. There is a mailing list, however at
`http://developer.berlios.de/mail/?group_id=769`.

Please remember to search the archives before posting a new message; it is likely that list members have already answered your question in the past.

Chapter 26

Customizing Linux

You can change *anything* on your Linux computer. One of the most common changes is the screen background, or "wallpaper," as some people call it. If you're an avid sailor, like this book's author, you might prefer a sunset over Longboat Key, as seen from the deck of your West Wight Potter sailboat, to the default *SimplyMEPIS* background.

When you use Linux for hassle-free computing, you have time to go sailing. Never forget: That's what all this is *about*! So let's start with a hassle-free screen background change.

Welcome to the KDE Control Center

This is where we do most of our customization. As you can see, it has a large number of categories, and their names are self-explanatory. To call up the Control Center, we go to the "System" section of our main menu, select "Settings," and choose "Control Center."

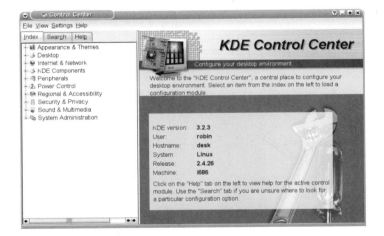

To change our desktop background we choose "Appearance and Themes" from the left-side "Control Center" menu, then click on "Background." You can choose "No Picture" if you like, and choose either solid colors or various patterns in

the lower half of the right side of the "Control Center" window. You can choose between a number of cleverly titled backgrounds in the gallery supplied by KDE that appears when you check "Picture." You can also choose a picture you have stored somewhere on your hard drive, as we did with that nice sunset photo. Just click on the folder icon between the "Pictures" menu and the box on the right side of the window where your chosen background shows as a preview so you can see how it will look on your screen. You can preview a dozen or a hundred pictures, decide which one you like best, then click "Apply" at the bottom of the screen to make that one your background. If you can't settle on just one, there's a "Slide Show" option you can choose. Click the "Setup" button next to the "Slide Show" check box and pick dozens of pictures that will show in either random or set order, changing from one to another as often as you choose.

Now here's the big trick, and it applies to almost every change you make through the KDE Control Center: You can revert to your previous setting or to the default setting with a single click, so experimentation is 100% risk-free.

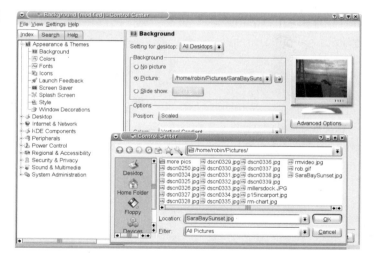

Other KDE appearance and behavior options work the same way as your

"Background" selection. Clicking buttons to see what they do is faster (and teaches you more) than reading about someone else doing it. We'll scan through a few of the more interesting options so you can get an idea of the amount of flexibility KDE gives you, but won't go deeply into each screen. You can click the "Help" tab on any Control Center screen and get a short explanation of what's going on, plus a link to a manual page that will give you full, often very geeky, explanations of what you're seeing and doing on the page where you clicked "Help."

Index | Search | Help

Fonts

This module allows you to choose which fonts will be used to display text in KDE. You can select not only the font family (for example, *helvetica* or *times*), but also the attributes that make up a specific font (for example, *bold* style and *12 points* in height.)

Just click the "Choose" button that is next to the font you want to change. You can ask KDE to try and apply font and color settings to non-KDE applications as well. See the "Style" control module for more information.

Use the "Whats This" (Shift+F1) to get help on specific options.

To read the full manual click <u>here</u>.

Multiple Desktops

This is a cool Linux trick you'll appreciate if you're in the habit of keeping many programs open at once. Down on your control panel at the bottom of the screen, near the middle, there's a little icon with the numbers "1" and "2" on it, one above the other. You're on desktop number one by default. If number one gets too crowded for you, instead of closing programs, you can click number two, and you have a fresh, uncluttered desktop.

You can display some program windows on one desktop and some on another. And if two desktops aren't enough for you, right-click on that icon and you'll see a window that will you to create up to 16 desktops—or space enough to hold 100 or more open program windows.

Right-Click for Fast Desktop Customization

We wanted to show you the KDE Control Center because it does more than configure the desktop, but for fast changes to your desktop appearance, right-click on any exposed desktop space (not covered by a program window—and if your desktop is completely covered, you can use the "Show Desktop" button next to the menu-opening K-Gear to clear it) to bring up a little menu box full of things you can do to your desktop. Click on them, play with them, and see what happens when you "Apply" your changes—just "Revert" or go back to "Defaults" if you don't like what you see.

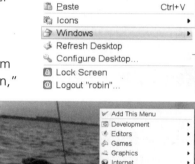

The panel behaves the same way; right-click anywhere on it and a menu pops up that gives you several choices, including the ability to add buttons that open programs to the panel so you don't need to go rooting around in the menu for ones you use all the time.

To add a new application button, click "Panel Menu." From there, choose "Add" and then choose "Application Button," which takes you to the same categorized list of programs you get by clicking the K-Gear icon. Click on the program you want to create an icon for, and it appears. If you want to move it, right-click on it, click on "Move (whatever) Button"—(whatever) being the name of the button you right-clicked on—and…move it. Want to remove it? Click "Remove Panel Button" and it's gone.

And if you remove it by mistake, you can always make a new one by going through the "Add" routine.

You can do many other things with the Panel configuration menu, too. Click "Configure Panel" and you can make it bigger or smaller, move it to the top of your screen, or have it show up vertically along either the left or right side. You can also make its background "transparent" so your desktop background shows through and replaces the default

207

industrial-looking gray, add sub-panels and little "Applets" that do things like give you constantly updated weather reports whenever you're connected to the Internet, and add a little blank where you can type or paste words and look them up in a dictionary. You can even create groups of miniature applications buttons in "Applet" form so you can click directly from your panel to every program you use regularly—and hardly ever use the K-Gear menu at all.

The Applet you add if you want lots of tiny application buttons is called "Quick Launcher." Put a Quick Launcher on your panel and

fill it with your favorite programs, change the clock style (by right-clicking on it, of course), and before you know it your panel will look completely different from how it did when you first started your computer with Linux.

Customizing Programs with Themes and Skins

Because many Linux aficionados delight in customizing their computers' appearances, it's natural that many popular programs for Linux can be "themed" to meet individual tastes. Mozilla is a prime example. From the top of a Mozilla window, click "Edit," choose "Preferences," click "Appearance" in the new window that brings up, and you have a number of choices. "Themes" gives you a chance to give your browser an entirely different look from its original factory-drab appearance; in fact, most of the Mozilla screenshots in this book are of the "Orbit" theme, which is one of the most popular ones around.

You can also change Mozilla colors, fonts (typefaces) and nearly everything else. And themes? You can change them like mad. There's a little "Get New Themes" link on the "Themes" page that takes you to a whole list of Internet sources (assuming you're connected at the time) for themes of all kinds, in colors ranging

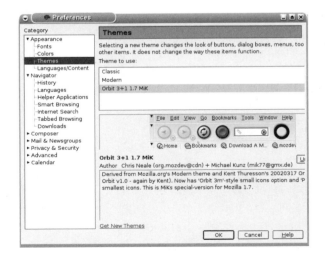

from subdued to garish. There are hundreds of Mozilla themes available. There are themes—or as they are sometimes called, "skins"—for OpenOffice.org, the XMMS media player, and most other popular Linux programs. Type the name of a favorite program and "skins" or "themes" into Google or another search engine, and you will usually find not only themes for it but also instructions on how to download and activate those themes, and often you'll find instructions on how to create your own themes from scratch.

There are people who spend endless hours turning their Linux desktops into works of art. Others are satisfied with the default appearance. Most of us are in between these two extremes: We want things to look nice, so we spend a few minutes now and then changing things around, but don't make a fetish of it. We're generally more function-oriented than art-oriented. So we spend at least some of our time discussing more practical matters than the search for the perfect desktop font.

Network Security and Networking

SimplyMEPIS includes a firewall that is activated automatically when you start it for the first time. The server software that is usually part of a Linux installation has intentionally been left out of *SimplyMEPIS* as a security measure, and your Guarddog firewall keeps the "ports" used to access those servers closed up tightly unless you choose to open them.

Every open port on a network connected computer gives bad hackers a potential point of entry. The port that allows VPN, while not considered a high security risk, is not open in *SimplyMEPIS* by default. In fact, the only ports that are open in your basic installation are the ones you need to send and receive email, view Web sites, download and upload files via ftp and several pop-

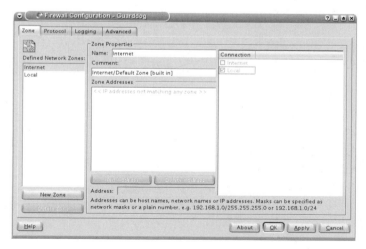

ular multimedia protocols, and those needed to use instant messaging services. You even need to open ports to use some popular file-sharing services. You can do this through the Guarddog control utility found in your "System" menu under the "Security" heading.

If you are not familiar with firewalls—or don't know why you need one—this is a good time to press that "Help" button. The Guarddog Handbook is one of the most complete pieces of documentation we've ever seen as part of an open source program. It's not only a guide to how Guarddog works, but a fine introduction to networking and network security in general. And, unlike many security tomes, it doesn't start out assuming you already know nearly everything, but leads you through networking and security procedures from the very beginning and gradually shows you more complex concepts as it goes along.

But you don't really need to read all this unless you want to (not that it would hurt) because Guarddog does a fine job of keeping your computer safe without doing anything at all to it. In fact, what you are most likely to do with Guarddog in a typical desktop situation is *open* ports, which *decreases* your security level slightly, although not enough that you should lose sleep over it.

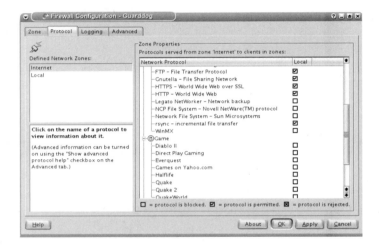

The "Protocols" window is where you do your port opening. You reach it by clicking the "Protocols" tab in the main Guarddog window. Note that none of these protocols for popular online games are currently enabled. This means that if you try to play these games, they will not work for you until you click them "open" and have a checkmark showing next to them (and not an "x" because that means your computer *specifically* rejects *that* protocol) and click "Apply" at the bottom of the window. The same goes for other protocols. If you can't make a network printer work from your MEPIS computer, you can't connect to a favorite file-sharing service or you have trouble making a VNC connection, the first thing to check is that you have the appropriate port open in Guarddog.

What are protocols and ports?

Protocols are methods of transferring information between computers over a local network or through the Internet.

They have names only an engineer could love, like HTTP (HyperText Transfer Protocol), FTP (File Transfer Protocol), CRTP (Combat Radio Transport Protocol), SSH (Secure Shell), and so on. Each one has a "Port Number" associated with it, like 80 for HTTP, which is how you get Web pages, and 1963 for MSN Messenger, and so on. There are thousands of possible ports. If they are all open on your PC, it means it will accept almost any kind of signal sent to it, including ones from bad people who want to steal your data or use your computer to send spam. If all the ports are closed, your computer won't accept any data, period.

So you keep some ports open by setting your firewall to allow certain signals through it, and in other cases (like HTTP), to allow signals in on that port only in response to signals it sends out.

Server computers—ones that "serve" Web pages, email, and other files to "client" computers like your desktop—*must* have some ports open so they can receive requests to send out Web pages or emails or whatever, so they can't be "locked down" as securely as a desktop computer. But some desktop computers become servers accidentally because their operating system packages came with built-in server software their owners don't know about. This is the most common security problem with Linux computers, and it's why *SimplyMEPIS* comes with no server software, although you can certainly *add* server software yourself if you need it.

The magic of a modern Linux distribution with a built-in firewall is that you don't need to know any of this stuff to set up your computer network and keep it secure. And, with Linux, you don't need to worry about all those Windows viruses, either. Just update your system now and then in case some sort of vulnerability in one of your programs has been spotted and fixed, and you can pretty much not worry about network security, but go to the beach instead.

Support for Other Languages

MEPIS is a U.S. creation, and its native language is English. But Linux and Linux software are international in nature, so it's easy to add additional language capabilities to MEPIS. In fact, there is a section in the MEPIS System Center that can help you add support for almost any major language to your Linux installation.

Here we have selected "Install Localizations," the two-letter code "it" (for Italian) has been chosen, and "KDE" is checked. Click "Install" and Italian translations for KDE will automatically download and install. Repeat this procedure for OpenOffice.org, Mozilla, and iSpell, and you'll have your largest programs "Italianized," along with your spellchecker. The only

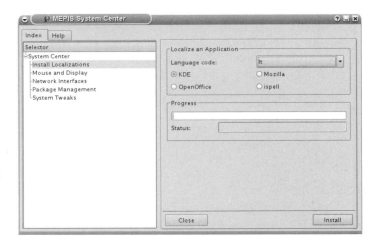

other step necessary to change languages is to go back to the KDE Control Center, select "Country/Region & Language," and change your keyboard setting and monetary units to meet your taste.

Finding non-English versions for other Linux programs is best done through online search engines. There are large repositories of MEPIS-compatible Debian programs in many languages, and the best place to find them is through search engine listings in your chosen language, not English.

Sharing Your Linux Computer

Your settings, including language, are yours. But you can give someone else access to your computer without sharing your settings by creating a separate login for them by clicking the K-Gear, then "System," then scrolling down to "KUser" and typing in your password when requested. This brings you to the User Manager screen, where you click the "Add User" icon to add a new user, although you may want to click "Help" first and learn how to control what you can allow your new user to do—and not do. This is especially useful if you are sharing your computer with a child and don't want to allow Internet use or other privileges unless you're there to watch.

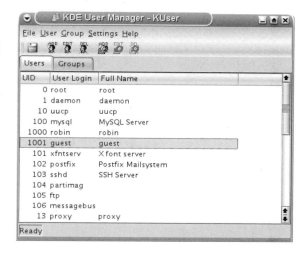

Where to Get Help

Customization and Administration

```
themes.freshmeat.net/kde
kde-look.org
docs.kde.org
kde-forum.org
mepis.org/forum
```

Security and Networking

```
debian.org/security
linuxsecurity.com
```

Chapter 27

Dipping a Toe Into the Command-line Waters

By Joe Barr

Don't be alarmed when you see the MEPIS command-line interface, AKA the CLI. You don't have to go there if you don't want to.

> ## Opening a command-line terminal
>
> To open a terminal window, click the K-Gear menu, go to the System submenu, and open Konsole. You now have full access to all Linux command-line functions.

With modern versions of Linux—like MEPIS—you very seldom if ever need to leave the ease and comfort of the GUI for your day-in, day-out computing chores. But if you ever need to, or if you just want to explore "under the hood" a bit, this chapter is for you. It provides a guide to twenty of the most useful commands available at the CLI. You can learn more about each of these commands simply by typing "man command-name" or "info command-name" in a console window.

alias

The alias command is very handy. It allows you to rename (sometimes long and intricate) commands to something a little easier to remember and type. How cool is that? You get to name commands whatever you like.

If it's hard for you to remember all the parameters to use to get a directory listing in a directory that shows all files and their permissions, ownership, and size, just use alias to call it, um, something familiar. How about "dir"?

In MEPIS, aliases are kept in a file called .bashrc, which lives in your home directory. Use KEdit to open .bashrc, and then enter the following line at the bottom:

```
alias fulldir='ls -al';
```

Then save the file.

Before you can use your new command, you have to log out and log back in. When you do, open a Konsole session and type your new command in it. You should see something like this:

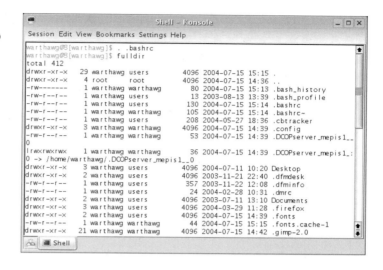

apropos

In those moments when my memory is not all it should be—when I can't recall the exact name of the command I need to do a task—it's good to know apropos.

The basic format for apropos is:

```
[username]$apropos search-term
```

Let's say you are searching for a command to edit sound files. To find all sound related commands, you would enter "apropos sound" at the command line. Here's what apropos had to say:

Anytime apropos found "sound" in its database, it told me the name of the program and gave brief description of it. At the bottom of that list I found sox, which allows you to translate sound files from one audio format to another, as well as add reverb or echo or other sound effects. Just what I was looking for.

```
warthawg@M[warthawg]$ apropos sound
QSound (3qt)            - Access to the platform audio facilities
artscat (1)            - pipe data to sound device
AuSoundCreateBucketFromData (3nas) - create a bucket and initialize its contents

AuSoundCreateBucketFromFile (3nas) - create a bucket and initialize its contents

AuSoundCreateDataFromBucket (3nas) - copy the data from a bucket into local memo
ry.
AuSoundCreateFileFromBucket (3nas) - copy the data from a bucket into a file.
AuSoundPlay (3nas)     - create a flow to play audio from any source.
AuSoundPlayFromBucket (3nas) - create a flow to play from a bucket.
AuSoundPlayFromData (3nas) - create a flow to play from memory.
AuSoundPlayFromFile (3nas) - create a flow to play a file.
AuSoundPlaySynchronousFromFile (3nas) - play a file.
AuSoundRecord (3nas) - create a flow to record audio to any destination.
AuSoundRecordToBucket (3nas) - create a flow to record to a bucket.
AuSoundRecordToData (3nas) - create a flow to record to memory.
AuSoundRecordToFile (3nas) - create a flow to record to a file.
AuSoundRecordToFileN (3nas) - (unknown subject)
AuSoundRecordToFileN (3nas) [AuSoundRecordToFileN] - (unknown subject)
cdda2wav (1)          - a sampling utility that dumps CD audio data into wav soun
d files
cdsound-recorder (1) - a direct-to-disk recorder wich uses a soundcard to recor
```

cal

The cal command, entered without any arguments, shows you a calendar for the current month that looks like this:

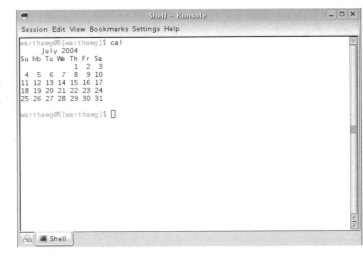

But there are several arguments you can add to the cal command to tell you even more. The Julian date, for example. Try this:

```
[username]$cal -j 1
2004
```

The previous example produces a rather normal looking calendar, but the -j argument changes it from showing the day of the month (1-31 for January) to the Julian date, or day of the year, instead. Of course for January, it's hard to tell the difference. Try this:

```
[username]$cal -j 2 2004
```

That lists month 2, with the days a little more obviously being day of the year rather than day of the month, as you can see here:

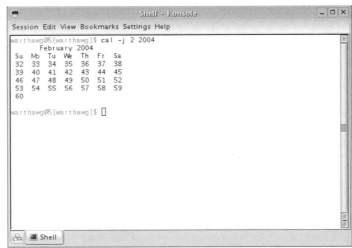

If you liked that, add a -y and cal will print the entire year for you. If you specify only a "-y" as an argument, cal will print a normal calendar for the entire year.

cat

The cat command (short for concatenate) is so handy that it's become famous for being used when it's not really needed. That must make the other shell commands green with envy. Some of them hardly ever get used.

Here's one way to abuse it. Say you want to look at the contents of a small text file. Just type "cat filename" at the command line and the text file will be printed in the console window.

When you want to combine two separate files into one, cat is the tool to use. The format is:

```
[username]$cat file1.name file2.name > combinedfile.name
```

Nothing to it, but note that the redirection symbol (the greater than symbol) overwrites any previous file of the same name you've specified for the output file. To add to an existing file instead of overwriting it, use two greater thans, like this:

```
[username]$cat file1.name file2.name >> combinedfile.name
```

There are more examples of using (and abusing) the cat command in the section on grep.

chmod

The chmod command allows you to change permissions for a file, or files, or a directory. Permissions determine whether you can read, write, or execute the file in question. Permissions are a big reason that Linux users are not as susceptible to email-borne viruses and trojans as Windows users, because most system files require *root* permission to use or change, and we never give our root password to virus-writers.

The basic format is: chmod NNN filename, where the first N represents the file owner's permissions, the second the file group's permissions, and the third everyone else's permissions. N can vary between 0 and 7. Here is a chart of the meaning of each:

N	READ	WRITE	EXECUTE
7	Y	Y	Y
6	Y	Y	N
5	Y	N	Y
4	Y	N	N
3	N	Y	Y
2	N	Y	N
1	N	N	Y
0	N	N	N

chown

The chown command is similar to chmod, but instead of altering file permissions, you can change the file's owner and group.

The basic format of the command is

```
[username]$chown owner.group filename
```

The group name is optional, so if you only want to change the owner, use "chown owner filename." If you only want to change the group, use the chgrp command instead.

cp

The basic format of the cp (short for copy) command is:

```
[username]$cp from-filename to-filename
```

Easy as pie. You can also copy directories as well as files, but if you do, be sure to use the "-R" (recursive) option so that you copy everything inside the directory. The command to fully copy a directory would be

```
[username]$cp -R from-dir to-dir
```

Let's copy a GIF file so that it has a file extension indicating that it's a JPEG image, and then see what the file command (which we'll look at it next) has to say about it. The format for the command to do that is

```
[username]$cp picture.gif trick-picture.jpg
```

It's been copied with the false name. To learn the consequences of doing so, see the section on the file command.

file

The file command gives you its best guess as to what kind of file the file you're asking about is. The format is simple, just enter:

```
[username]$file filename
```

In response, file tells you everything it can about what type of file "filename" is. This response, by the way, is not based on anything as simplistic as a file type or extension. If you name a graphics image "image.txt," for example, file won't mistakenly tell you that it's a text file. Or if you rename an executable trojan "image.jpg," file won't tell you it's a graphic image. This is a good thing. Lots of bad things happen in the land of DOS/Windows because people are fooled by a file extension.

Now about that phony trick-picture.jpg we created with copy. Will file be fooled by the file extension? Not a chance. If you enter

```
[username]$file trick-picture.jpg
```

File will respond with this:

```
trickpicture.jpg: GIF image data, version 89a, 640 x 480
```

Pretty cool. It even gives you the size of the image.

find

Find is one of the most sophisticated and complex commands available to you. What it actually does—find files that match its search parameters—is simple. The devil is in the parameters. We'll limit our discussion here to quick and easy searches.

The format is as follows:

```
[username]$find searchpath search-parameters
```

The searchpath argument defines the scope of the search. If you only want to look in your current directory and all the directories beneath it, you would use "." as the searchpath, like this:

```
[username]$find . search-parameters
```

If you wanted to look everywhere, you would use this:

```
[username]$find / search-parameters
```

Let's say you want to find a file called personal.data, and you are not sure where it is. To search the entire system, you would use:

```
[username]$find / -name personal-data
```

Note that the search-parameter option used is "-name." Any files matching that name (personal-data.xml, personal-data.txt, etc) will be listed.

grep

The grep command searches the files you specify for the pattern you specify. It's very handy for finding things inside regular text files. The basic format of the command is this:

```
grep (options) pattern file1 file2 ...
```

Each match found is displayed, unless otherwise specified. The options make the command a lot handier. You can make it case insensitive by specifying "-i", or simply count the number of times the pattern is found instead of printing them by specifying "-c". If you simply wish to know which files contain the search pattern, use the "-l" option.

I have a large text file containing names and phone numbers, and I never remember if I have entered the names upper and lowercase, or just lower. When I want to find my friend Steve's work number, I use grep this way:

```
[username]$grep -i steve phones.txt
```

more (or less)

There is a very handy program included in most Linux distributions called more. It's used to display the contents of a text file one page at a time, rather than simply dumping the entire file to the terminal. If you recall, that's what the cat command does, and if you need information at the top of a file that's more than a page long, you have to read real fast to get it.

The command format is simple, just enter

```
[username]$more filename
```

Scrolling a page at a time is a step in the right direction, but it's not all that. What happens when you go a page or two further, then find you need to go back? Scroll bars on your terminal window may get you back to where you want to be, but more won't. That's one case where less is more.

There is a similar, but more advanced, program called less. It does everything more can do, and more. Most importantly, it allows you to go backward and forward as you browse. If you are used to using more and can't remember to type less instead, you might want to create an alias to remember for you. Like this:

```
[username]$alias more='less'
```

Less, in this case, is definitely more.

locate

The locate command is similar to find in its use, but the search is performed in an entirely different way. Locate searches through a database that is recreated by the updatedb program and is usually run once a day. Well, make that once a night, instead.

So the bad news you need to be aware of when using the locate command is that files created since the last time updatedb was run will not appear in its search results. The good news is that it runs very quickly, much faster than find does.

The basic format for the locate command is

```
locate pattern
```

Like the grep command, locate will let you specify to case-insensitivity when matching the pattern. That can be very helpful at times.

ls

The ls (short for list) command is the Linux equivalent of dear old DOS's dir command. Of course, ls is much more powerful and sophisticated than its cousin from Redmond, but that goes without saying.

The basic format of the command is

```
ls [options]... file-or-directory-names
```

Without any options, the command produces a list of file names in alphabetical order for either the current directory or the directories.

Of course, there may be "hidden" files in that directory. To find out, we need to add an option to show all. You do that by adding the "-a" option, like this:

```
[username]$ls -a
file-or-directory-
name
```

If we add another option, the "-l" for long form, the look of directory listing changes considerably. Try "ls -al" from the command line. You should get something that looks like this:

```
                                                         Shell – Konsole                        _ □ X
Session Edit View Bookmarks Settings Help
-rw-r--r--      1 warthawg warthawg    39470 2004-07-15 15:18 mepis-cli-02.png
-rw-r--r--      1 warthawg warthawg    39927 2004-07-15 15:19 mepis-cli-03.png
-rw-r--r--      1 warthawg warthawg    21365 2004-07-15 15:21 mepis-cli-04.png
-rw-r--r--      1 warthawg warthawg    22228 2004-07-15 15:28 mepis-cli-05.png
drwxr-xr-x      3 warthawg users         4096 2004-05-26 20:31 .mplayer
drwxr-xr-x      2 warthawg users         4096 2004-03-14 10:44 Music
-rw-------      1 warthawg users         1102 2004-05-27 18:36 mycheckbook
-rw-r--r--      1 warthawg users         1102 2004-05-27 18:36 mycheckbook.backup
drwxr-xr-x      3 warthawg users         4096 2004-05-24 13:24 News
drwxr-xr-x      2 warthawg users         4096 2004-03-12 15:33 Pictures
drwxr-xr-x      2 warthawg users         4096 2003-01-28 18:51 public_html
drwxr-xr-x      2 warthawg users         4096 2004-07-15 14:39 .qt
drwxrwxrwx      2 warthawg users         4096 2003-09-03 23:06 Shared
drwxr-xr-x      2 warthawg users         4096 2004-05-22 15:22 smb4k
drwxr-xr-x      2 warthawg users         4096 2003-07-13 08:15 .spamassassin
drwx------      2 warthawg warthawg     4096 2004-07-15 14:41 .ssh
drwxr-xr-x      2 warthawg users         4096 2004-05-24 13:24 .straw
drwx------      3 warthawg warthawg     4096 2004-07-15 14:39 .thumbnails
drwxr-xr-x      2 warthawg users         4096 2002-12-10 15:34 tmp
drwxr-xr-x      2 warthawg users         4096 2003-11-16 17:23 .tuxracer
-rw-r--r--      1 warthawg users          492 2003-11-16 17:42 .xawtv
drwxr-xr-x      3 warthawg users         4096 2004-05-24 13:24 .xine
-rw-------      1 warthawg warthawg   236541 2004-07-15 15:28 .xsession-errors
warthawg@5[warthawg]$ []
 Δ   ■ Shell
```

The first column indicates whether the file is a directory or not. If it is, a "d" appears there. If not, it's an "-." Next come three columns indicating the read, write, and execute (by showing an r, w, or x if the function is allowed) for the file owner. Next come three more columns showing the same information for the file group. Then three that show permissions for everyone else. Then come the file size, the date and time it was created, and the file name.

mv

Let's say we decide to keep all our JPEGs in one directory and all our GIFs in another. Our task now is to remove the clutter from the directory we've been working in by putting those files where they belong—all except for the trick-picture.jpg, that is. We'll just delete that.

The mv command follows the same basic format as cp:

```
[username]$mv from-filename to-filename
```

Our cleanup chore requires us to move the files to different directories, however, so we need to add the directory information to the "to-filename" to get it in the right place. For file operations in the local directory, of course, we don't need to specify the full directory. The directory path is assumed to be the same unless otherwise specified. This is the otherwise case.

I've been working in my home directory, /home/warthawg. To get the JPEG put up in its proper place, I will need to move it to the /home/warthawg/jpg directory. One way to use the mv command to do that looks like this:

```
[username]$mv picture.jpg /home/warthawg/jpg/picture.jpg
```

I could have also used

```
[username]$mv picture.jpg jpg/picture.jpg
```

That one works because, by not putting a "/" in front of the "jpg" directory name, I have indicated that it resides in the current directory.

rm

The rm command removes files and directories. Use it with extreme caution—you do not want to accidentally remove a file your computer needs to function.

The basic format is

```
rm filename
```

A safer format for the rm command is to use it with the "-i" option, like this:

```
[username]$rm -i filename
```

The "-i" tells rm that you want to confirm each deletion before it's done.

To remove entire directories, use the "-rf" options. But do it very carefully. The "-r" option tells rm to recursively remove files and directories found within the directory being deleted. The "-f" tells rm to do it without question or complaint.

su

The su command is magic. It allows you to assume the rights and privileges of root, the "super user." Provided you know the root password, of course. As root, you will have supreme permissions on the system, not just to look in files and directories of any other users, but to execute programs mere mortals cannot. It's normally used in two ways: to become root, or to become another user.

To become root, simply type

```
[username]$su
```

at the command line and then enter the root password when asked.

You'll know you're root when the $ becomes a #, like this:

```
[username]#
```

To end the "super user" session, type

```
[username]#exit
```

To become another user, use this:

```
[username]$su username
```

Then provide that user's password when asked. Escaping from your alternate-identity session is the same as from root, just "exit."

tar

Tar (an abbreviation of tape archive) provides the means to make, compress and decompress archives. Archive in this sense means that many different, separate files can be combined into a single file. We call that file the tarball. Keep in mind that the compression is an optional, separate task. You can create and "melt" tarballs without compressing the data at all.

The basic format of the tar command is

```
tar (options)   filename-1 ...
```

To create a tarball containing everything in a directory named "text" in my home directory, I would enter from the command line in my home directory the following command:

```
[username]$tar -cf textarchive.tar text
```

The "-c" option tells tar to create an archive, the "f" tells it to use the following name as the name for the archive it creates.

The first name given in the previous example becomes the name of the archive. Note that you can name it anything you like, but the more meaningful you make the name, the easier it will be to handle the tarball later. The ".tar" extension indicates it is an uncompressed tarball.

Here are a few other standard tarball extensions:

.tar.gz—a "gunzip" compressed tarball
   .tgz—also a "gunzip" compressed tarball
   .tar.bz2—a "bunzip2" compressed tarball

Why is it important to indicate the type of compression used? Good question. The answer is that when you "melt" the tarball, you need to know which decompression program to use. There are two ways to handle compressed tarballs, the long way and the short way.

The long way is to decompress it first, then use tar to "melt" the tarball back into its original component files. Let's say we have a tar archive named "bigarchive.tgz." We could do it in two steps, like this:

```
[username]$gunzip -d bigarchive.tgz
```

The archive would now appear with the name of bigarchive.tar instead of bigarchive.tgz, since we told gunzip to decompress it with the "-d" option. Next step is this:

```
[username]$tar -xf bigarchive.tar
```

That would "melt" the tarball and all the original files would be present again.

Or we could do it all in one step, by adding the "z" option to our tar command, telling it that the archive to be melted is in gunzip compression format.

```
[username]$tar -xzf bigarchive.tgz
```

If our original file had been compressed with bunzip2 instead of gunzip—we would know this if it was correctly named with the .bz2 extension—we would use the "j" option for tar instead of the "z," like this:

```
[username]$tar -xjf bigarchive.bz2
```

Note that the first option in all three cases is "x", meaning to extract the files from the archive. When we create the tarballs, the first option is "c."

227

Sometimes it is handy to know exactly what is in an archive before you melt it. You can list the contents of a tarball by changing that first option to "t." If the archive is compressed, however, you still have to tell tar that it is, using the "z" or "j" option as noted previously.

test

The test command allows you to conditionally perform some task based on the existence, type, or status of a file. It also lets you do the same thing by comparing integer and string values. For my sake, we'll keep it as simple as possible and stick to file tests while still showing off some of its potential.

The command here tests for the existence of /var/mail/username (that's what the -e argument does) *and* sounds a beep if it is found.

```
[username]$test -e /var/spool/mail/username && cat
/usr/share/sounds/KDE_Beep_Beep.wav >/dev/dsp
```

Note the "&&" operator in the command above, separating the test command from the cat command. That's a logical AND operator, which requires both sides of the command to be true or else it won't execute. If the /var/spool/mail/username file does not exist, the test won't be true and the beep won't sound.

What if you want to hear the beep only when you don't have mail? Cool. Not a problem. Just add a NOT operator in front of the -e argument. The ! mark is the NOT operator, so our revised test command would look like this:

```
[username]$test ! -e /var/spool/mail/username &&  cat
/usr/share/sounds/KDE_Beep_Beep.wav >/dev/dsp
```

In addition to testing for the existence of a file, you can test to see if a file is a directory by using the -d argument, or to see if it exists and contains data by using the -s argument, or many other optional tests.

In our case, the username file remains in existence even after your mail client has removed the mail. That means our test with the "-e" option is meaningless, because it will always be true whether you actually have mail or not. What we really want to use is the "-s" option, which ensures the file size is greater than zero, like this: `[username]$test -s /var/spool/mail/username && echo "You have mail"`

Command-line Help

`www.mepis.org/forum` is full of command-line gurus.

`www.linux.com` has many valuable command line tips.

`www.tldp.org` (The Linux Documentation Project) is a huge compendium of command line instructions.

Appendix C, "Books that Can Help You Become More Proficient with Linux," lists several references that will help you become totally competent with the Linux command line.

Chapter 28

Joining the Linux Community

Unlike Windows, Mac OS, and most other commercial operating systems, Linux is not owned by a single company. It was developed—and is constantly being improved—by a worldwide group of programmers who are more interested in technical elegance than marketing. These programmers are usually not hobbyists, but academics, professional software developers, and others who use Linux on their own computers and, increasingly, in their employers' information technology (IT) departments. Linux is one of the most outstanding instances of international and inter-corporate cooperation the world has ever seen, as are the Free Software and Open Source communities that have grown up around it.

How GNU/Linux Got Started

Your new operating system's real name is GNU/Linux. "Linux" is its nickname, used in everyday conversation the same way the late U.S. president Dwight David Eisenhower was called "Ike" in newspaper headlines and almost everywhere else. The GNU (pronounced "guh-noo") part of GNU/Linux is the foundation on which the rest is built, a software system and development philosophy that was conceived in the early 1980s by Richard M. Stallman, an employee of the M.I.T. Artificial Intelligence Lab. At the time, Unix was the dominant operating system on the lab's larger computers, but each computer ran its own proprietary version of Unix, supplied by its manufacturer, so it was nearly impossible to use a printer or other device supplied by one manufacturer with a computer supplied by another. And because each of these Unix variants was owned by the company that sold it or included it with its hardware, Stallman couldn't write "bridge" programs to allow different devices to work with each other unless he signed non-disclosure agreements with all the different computer and device manufacturers involved. That would have kept him from freely sharing any of their secrets—or his own software that made use of their proprietary computer code—with other programmers and computer administrators who might also need it. Perhaps Stallman could have signed some of those non-disclosure agreements and contracted with computer vendors to write proprietary software for them, but he decided, instead, that it would be better to develop an operating system and software that could be used, modified, and shared by anyone, anywhere, without the licensing frustrations that typically accompanied proprietary software.

Early on, Stallman identified and started promoting four basic principles of software freedom:

1. You have the freedom to run the program, for any purpose.
2. You have the freedom to modify the program to suit your needs. (To make this freedom effective in practice, you must have access to the source code, because making changes in a program without having the source code is exceedingly difficult.)
3. You have the freedom to redistribute copies, either gratis or for a fee.
4. You have the freedom to distribute modified versions of the program, so that the community can benefit from your improvements.

Note that the word "free" in "Free Software" is about freedom, not price. Stallman sold copies of GNU Emacs (a programmers' text and code editor), one of the first programs distributed under a GNU license, for $150. Of course, because buyers were free to share their copies with friends and coworkers, sales revenue was not as high as it might have been if Stallman had required each user to purchase a copy. But in return for less income per copy, Stallman's program not only was shared so heavily both physically (on tapes, floppy disks, and other media) but over the then-tiny Internet that tens of thousands of programmers who might not have had money to buy their own copies got in the habit of using it, and many of those programmers took advantage of their freedom to *modify* the program, so GNU Emacs was improved and had features added at a much greater rate than Stallman could have managed on his own.

Note that because all Emacs users shared the freedom to modify and redistribute its under-lying code, all Emacs users got all the improvements made by any one user. Stallman ended up with a far better text and code editor for his own use than he would have if he'd sold Emacs as proprietary software.

In 1985, Stallman and others incorporated the Free Software Foundation (FSF) as a tax-exempt charity. The FSF soon released a number of essential software tools, including the widely-used GCC computer code compiler and the BASH "shell" (for command line utilities) under their GNU "copyleft" license that incorporated the four freedoms mentioned previously, plus clauses that prevented anyone from using "copyleft" code in proprietary software so that their modifications to the original software could not be freely shared.

Many proprietary software companies denounced this clause in what soon became known as the "General Public License" (GPL) for software, because they felt they should have the right to appropriate others' work, add their own to it, and profit from the result instead of sharing their improvements (or profits) with the software's original creators.

Proprietary software vendors make their money by keeping their software's inner workings secret, not by sharing it, and get bent out of shape when others don't want to follow the same pattern. In fact, Stallman's rejection of the proprietary Unix software distribution pattern has a lot to do with the name GNU, which is an acronym for "Gnu's Not Unix." This is not just a statement of programming philosophy, but a programmer's joke: recursive statements that lead to endless circular discussions can bring improperly programmed computers to a halt.

Imagine a computer engaged in this dialogue:

"What is GNU?"

"GNU's Not Unix."

"What is GNU?"

"GNU's Not Unix."

"What is GNU?"

"GNU's Not Unix."

"What is GNU?"

"GNU's Not Unix."

This could go on forever—or at least until a human comes along and pulls the plug.

As comedian Jeff Foxworthy might say, "If you think this joke is funny… you just might be a programmer." (And if you think it's funny and you're *not* a programmer, perhaps you should consider becoming one.)

Enter Linus Torvalds

In 1991, a computer science student in Finland wrote a simple program so he could run his home computer the way a Unix-like operating system called Minix would. It was a rough little "kernel" program that only performed a few basic functions; by no means a complete operating system. But what few things this little program did, it did well, and Torvalds put his computer code on the Internet so others could use and perhaps improve it, along with this introductory message posted in the comp.os.minix Usenet NewsGroup:

```
Hello everybody out there using minix -

I'm doing a (free) operating system (just a hobby, won't be big
and professional like gnu) for 386(486) AT clones. This has been
brewing since april, and is starting to get ready. I'd like any
feedback on things people like/dislike in minix, as my OS resem-
bles it somewhat (same physical layout of the file-system (due to
practical reasons) among other things).
```

```
I've currently ported bash(1.08) and gcc(1.40), and things seem
to work. This implies that I'll get something practical within a
few months, and I'd like to know what features most people would
want. Any suggestions are welcome, but I won't promise I'll
implement them :-)

                Linus (torvalds@kruuna.helsinki.fi)

PS. Yes - it's free of any minix code, and it has a multi-
threaded fs. It is NOT portable (uses 386 task switching etc),
and it probably never will support anything other than AT-hard-
disks, as that's all I have :-(.
```

This message is commonly held up as the beginning of "Linux," a name suggested by Torvalds' friend Ari Lemmke as an alternative to Torvalds' own "Freax" name for his little program. Even renamed, Linux only became a usable operating system after others—many others—took Linus up on his invitation to submit suggestions, plus incorporation of many GNU tools. By 1993 GNU/Linux was on its way to success, with thousands of devotees contributing modifications and suggestions, the best of which Torvalds incorporated into the Linux kernel. And as Linux's popularity and usefulness grew, thousands of other programmers in dozens of countries started writing software designed specifically to run on the GNU/Linux operating system.

The Linux Community and You

When you start using Linux you become part of the Linux community. You get to paste stickers showing Tux, the Linux penguin mascot, on your computer, and put little Tux dolls on top of your bookself. This—along with going to Linux conferences—is the fun part of the Linux community. And yes, even though Linux is a dead-serious computer operating system, there is nothing wrong with being lighthearted about it. Linus Torvalds called his autobiography *Just for the Fun of It*, and this attitude pervades much Linux and free software development.

"Why not enjoy your computer work?" is the perennial rhetorical question behind Linux. "Sure," Linux seems to say, "You have 28 reports to turn out by the end of the week, but shouldn't you be able to stop and look at a pretty desktop picture and play a round of *Frozen Bubble* now and then? Shouldn't you move your KDE Control Panel from the bottom of your monitor screen to the top for no reason other than to keep from getting bored? Shouldn't you have a silly penguin mascot for your operating system?"

Well, yes. You should. Your computer should be your friend, not your enemy, and the programmers who write the software that runs it should be interested in how their programs work for you, and should be happy to listen to your suggestions about how they can improve their work. And most of them are. As long as you approach them politely, and take the trouble to read their manuals and documentation and FAQs (Frequently Asked Questions) before you ask for help, you'll find that most free software developers are happy to have your input and will often act on your suggestions much faster than commercial software companies that need to run every customer suggestion through twenty layers of customer service, legal, and marketing bureaucracies before they can decide if they even want to listen to you, let alone actually do anything.

There are public email lists and IRC channels for almost every free Linux program, and hundreds of them for Linux itself. You are welcome to join any of them and make suggestions or—if you are a programmer—contribute modifications. If your modifications are useful, they will probably be adopted whether you are a professional programmer working at one of IBM's Linux labs or a teenager using a public computer terminal in a Brazilian slum, and if they aren't useful they will be rejected even if you are a computer science professor who has written a dozen books on programming.

This meritocracy and willingness to listen to users among free software developers may scare old-fashioned proprietary software vendors, but from our perspective as users, it is wonderful because it give us better software faster, often for little or no cash outlay. Why should we care if one of the authors of our favorite program lives in Kenya and wears robes, while another lives in London and wears tailored suits? With the Internet as the primary collaboration medium for free software developers, it is possible to build ad-hoc coalitions of programmers who live on different continents and come together to create software that benefits everyone, everywhere.

Profiting from free software

The first thing to remember when someone asks, "How does anyone make a living writing free software?" is that there is nothing wrong with charging for free software; the "free" here is about freedom, not price. The second thing to remember is that most software is not written for mass-market distribution but is custom software produced for corporate and government clients who have very specific needs and hire programmers to fill them. More and more, companies and government agencies that need software written to their specifications look for programmers who have actively contributed to free software projects because hiring managers can look at the actual code those programmers have written and evaluate its quality.

Imagine yourself as a hiring manager choosing between two applicants. One has a resume that says, "I worked for XCorp on the YSoft project for two years." The other's resume says, "I have worked on three KDE projects. Please download and evaluate the code I wrote. You can find it at dot.kde.dot." You can not only look at your KDE developer's actual work, but also use a search engine to find archived posts he or she has made to the email lists for the projects on which he or she has worked to get an idea of that programmer's ability to interact with other team members and end users. Given a choice, hiring manager, you are going to chose the person who is a known quantity; someone whose work and work interactions are open for you to view instead of hidden behind a proprietary veil.

If you are contracting a development task to an outside firm, the same rules apply: You have a choice between companies that do proprietary work and can't show you what they've done for other clients and companies that do open source or free software work you can evaluate for yourself. ("Open Source" is a somewhat broader term than "Free Software," and can apply to software licensed under terms not sanctioned by the Free Software Foundation but that preserve Stallman's original "four freedoms.")

Another hiring and contracting pattern we're seeing with growing frequency is companies and government agencies that make direct use of free or open source programs, but need them customized to meet their specific requirements. Who better to hire for the customization than the people who developed those programs in the first place?

In addition to these advantages, open source and free software programmers don't need to pay license fees to use Linux as their underlying operating system or pay royalties to a program's original developers in order to use their work——as long as they share any published modifications or improvements with those original developers and other users of the software, which gives them a huge competitive cost advantage over proprietary software developers—plus the fact that they get to take advantage of others' modifications in return for contributing their own back into the "pool" so they can often produce software not only for less money but significantly faster than proprietary competitors.

We mentioned bug reports and feature suggestions as ways ordinary users (non-programmers) can contribute to free and open source software development, but there are many other ways to help. Art is an excellent example. Someone needs to make the logos and design the screen layouts and generally work to make the software they use look nice. Help files and manuals don't write themselves. Someone needs to write them—and edit them and update them as the software itself evolves.

Then there's translation. If Farsi is your native language and there is no Farsi version of your favorite text editor, why not do the translation yourself? With free and open source software you aren't going to violate anyone's copyrights. If you tell the program's developers what you're doing they aren't going to get angry, but are likely to offer you help and encouragement. After all, more users—Farsi-speakers—means more bug reports and more potential developers to pitch in and improve the project for everyone, no matter what language they speak, not to mention expanded commercial possibilities if the program's original developers also write custom software based on their open source development work, as so many do.

You can also help your favorite Linux distribution or free software project by publicizing it. Proprietary software companies spend millions promoting their wares, but many worthwhile open source programs get little or no attention, even if they work beautifully, because no one bothers to send out press announcements when new versions are released or take any one of a dozen other simple steps that might let people know that software is available. Most programmers are more interested in programming than in sending email to computer publication editors or performing other marketing-type tasks, so many worthwhile pieces of free software don't get the attention they deserve. If you find that a particular program is valuable to you, chances are it will also be valuable to others. A few emails to software reviewers might help spread word of your favorite program—and while you're at it, you might even want to send a simple "Thank you for your efforts" email to the program's developers. Sometimes a bit of appreciation is as valuable as money—not that money or equipment donations are a bad thing to offer, although you may be surprised to learn that many (but far from all) free software authors will turn down donation offers because they are either writing free software as part of their jobs or are doing it because they enjoy creating quality programs as an art form and simply aren't interested in earning money from it.

Linux Beyond the Desktop

Even though the first Linux kernel was written on (and for) a student's desktop computer, it has found more acceptance (so far) as a commercial operating system than on desktop PCs. Linux runs in the background everywhere from stock exchanges to giant Internet search engines like Google. Over half of the world's 500 most powerful supercomputers run Linux. At least 25% of all Web sites (including some of the world's most popular ones) are hosted on Linux servers.

Most major motion picture studios use Linux for animation and special effects production. Indeed, you can download and install CinePaint, a program used to create special effects for Harry Potter movies (and many others) and run it on your Linux computer at home. It will probably run too slowly for professional use on your computer, and no piece of software can give you talent, but at least the tool is available to you—for free, no less.

Linux has been loaded successfully on devices ranging from computerized wristwatches up
to top-of-the-line mainframe computers. A TiVo personal video recorder is essentially a Linux computer that's limited to only a few functions and is controlled by a few buttons instead of a keyboard.

An increasing number of industrial controllers and other devices you don't think of as "computers" run stripped-down embedded versions of Linux, too. In fact, the desktop computer is almost the last computing frontier Linux hasn't either conquered outright or at least started moving rapidly toward dominating, although even that table looks like it is starting to turn. Companies are starting to test Linux on desktop (and laptop) computers used by employees ranging from sales clerks to oil refinery engineers, and every year the rate of desktop Linux adoption seems to increase slowly but surely.

"Familiar with desktop Linux and common Linux programs including Mozilla and OpenOffice.org" is already a good statement to put on your resume, because it shows you have enough initiative to rise above the common computing herd, and as Linux keeps spreading through the corporate world, Linux knowledge is going to become more and more valuable when you're trying to get a new job (or a promotion).

Joining or Starting a Linux Users Group (LUG)

There are LUGs all over the world, with memberships as small as three or four and as large as three or four thousand.

Suncoast Linux Users Group
www.suncoastlug.org

This book's author belongs to the Suncoast Linux Users Group (SLUG), which is based in Tampa, Florida, and holds meetings in a number of towns outside of Tampa as well.

SLUG has an active email list where you can ask and answer technical questions. SLUG members range from "I just installed Linux on this computer" to professional systems administrators and programmers, including more than a few who have advanced degrees in engineering, computer science, and other technical disciplines. And SLUG is not an extraordinary LUG in any way, but rather a very typical one, much like its counterparts everywhere from San Francisco to New Delhi.

LUG meeting formats vary—sometimes there are formal presentations and sometimes there aren't—but no one has ever stopped a member from bringing a troublesome PC to a meeting and asking others to help get it working right or for help getting a troublesome piece of specialized or experimental software installed on it. Your LUG is a great source of Linux help whether you're a new user or you're a computer-savvy meteorologist who has been running Linux since 1994, and you're building a 2000-node supercomputing cluster so you can make accurate hurricane predictions by running real-time climate simulation programs that take millions of variables into account. Even if you only get to LUG meetings rarely (or not at all), LUG email lists are almost always great places to get fast, direct, one-on-one answers to Linux questions, and you don't need to be in the same city or town as the nearest LUG to join its email list. There are typically no dues or other formal requirements for LUG membership. You just show up, either in person or on the email list, and there you are. You can find a rather good online list of LUGs at `lugww.counter.li.org`. As of July 2004, it showed 647 groups in 91 countries, with the number increasing every month. That page also contains links to several others that will teach you how to start your own LUG, something that takes organizational rather than technical skill.

Perhaps, if you are an organizer-type person rather than a technically inclined one, starting a LUG will be your contribution to the Linux community. If you do, remember that Linux is supposed to be fun, so there should be a social component to your group that goes beyond technical training and support. Most Linux users are just like you: intelligent, aware people who have many interests beyond computing, even if some of them are a little shy when they're not sitting in front of their keyboards. Get them together in a social situation—perhaps including wives or husbands, children or parents, and a few coworkers or cousins who tag along—and you can usually put together a pretty good picnic or other event.

This book's author is a regular at the monthly SLUG "social meetings" typically held at the Cock and Bull Pub in Sarasota, Florida. In fact, much though he hates to admit it, he goes to more "social" LUG meetings than "real" ones, because many of the technical subjects discussed in the real meetings are over his head.

There's Always More to Learn About Linux

Even if you find yourself scratching your head a little at first or need to get a little help to make your first Linux installation run properly, before long you'll find Linux so familiar that if you go back to whatever operating system you were using before you discovered Linux, you'll get frustrated with its limitations.

Take it from one who knows.

Linux can be both frustrating and wonderful. The frustrating part is that solving some Linux problems can seem unbearably tedious the first time you tackle them. The wonderful thing is that you *can solve* almost any Linux problem, including problems that can't possibly be solved in other operating systems because you aren't allowed to tinker with their inner workings. Not long after you start using Linux you may find yourself saying, "If only I could do…" and asking questions on your LUG email list and doing Web searches until you find a way to do it either by clicking *here* and then clicking *there* or by making a command-line entry or two. You get all full of pride. You fixed something on your own you thought would be too hard for you to figure out. You are a Linux Wizard!

Then you think of something else you'd like to do with Linux, perhaps something you never tried to do with your computer before, and you know you're a Linux Wizard so you know you can figure it out—except this time maybe it's not so easy, so you do more research and learn how to write a command-line script to accomplish your objective, possibly even learn a little Perl (or another scripting language) along the way.

You are now in serious trouble.

Now that you have learned a little about how your computer works, and how to *change* the way it works, there will be no stopping you. If you go to a LUG meeting and somebody says, "You can increase system performance by adding RAM," you'll want to take your computer apart and add more RAM (Random Access Memory) to it, even if you're never looked inside it before and have no idea what RAM looks like or how to add it.

Because you have now gotten the idea, through learning Linux, that your computer is something you can figure out and work on yourself, instead of saying "Oh, I don't know much about computers," you'll ask questions and prowl search engines, and learn what RAM is and how to add it to your computer. And after you've conquered RAM, how about upgrading that video card? What about optimizing your Linux kernel to gain just a tiny bit more performance?

This can go on and on, until the day comes at work or school when someone else's computer isn't working right, and you know exactly why—and you tell them. You will be cast as the local computer expert forevermore, and if you're not careful you may drift into systems administration or programming instead of staying a normal, happy person.

Not that there's anything wrong with that...

Robin 'Roblimo' Miller
Bradenton, Florida, 2004

Section IV

Appendices

Guide to Other Popular Linux Distributions

MEPIS is but one of many Linux distributions. The ten Linux desktop distributions listed here were the most popular English-language ones— besides MEPIS—recorded by www.distrowatch.com in July 2004.

Mandrake Linux

This was the first Linux distribution that worked hard to make Linux easy for ordinary desktop users. The company that produces it, MandrakeSoft, has had many ups and downs since it was founded in 1998, and some of their releases have had quality control problems, but Mandrake Linux is now stable and workable for users at all levels, not just beginners.

`www.mandrakelinux.com`

The Fedora Project

This is a community-developed, freely downloadable distribution that replaces the old no-charge version of Red Hat Linux but is still sponsored and supported by Red Hat. It is generally targeted more toward hobbyists and experimenters than desktop computer users.

`(fedora.redhat.com)`

Knoppix

A bootable CD with a collection of GNU/Linux software, automatic hardware detection, and support for many graphics cards, sound cards, SCSI and USB devices and other peripherals. It is similar to MEPIS in many ways, and will sometimes work with "oddball" hardware that give MEPIS trouble, but is somewhat harder to install on your hard drive.

`(www.knoppix.com)`

The Debian Project

Debian is a true free (in both sense of the word) software project and it's the one on which MEPIS is based. Debian is generally command-line-oriented, but has some GUI system tools available.

`(www.debian.org)`

SUSE Linux

SUSE is a division of enterprise networking leader Novell, Inc., and while there is a downloadable version of SUSE available, you must purchase a copy to get some of SUSE's proprietary system tools, and license restrictions prohibit sharing these tools. SUSE places a heavy emphasis on corporate sales, but is excellent for individual desktop users, too. It's a well-integrated package, suitable for new and experienced users.

(www.suse.com)

Slackware Linux

One of the oldest continuously-published Linux distributions, aimed at hobbyists and Linux sophisticates, not desktop users. You will use the command line quite a bit if you run Slackware.

(www.slackware.com)

Gentoo Linux

A completely free Linux distribution geared towards developers and network professionals that uses a unique package management system called Portage instead of the more common RPM and DEB systems.

(www.gentoo.org)

Xandros

An excellent desktop distribution based on the old Corel Linux OS. Debian-based, works well, easy to install and upgrade. There's an "Open Circulation" edition available for free download, but if you want all the bells and whistles (and a manual) you'll need to spend close to $100 for the full-featured "Deluxe" edition. Restrictive license limits sharing.

(www.xandros.com)

PCLinuxOS

A rather new Live CD distribution initially based on Mandrake Linux but rapidly coming into its own. Has attractive default and utility screens.

(www.pclinuxonline.com/pclos)

Linspire

Features simple basic installation and easy installation of additional software. Most Linspire software is the same software you find in other Linux distributions with changed names, and it is not obvious how to switch from Linspire's Click-N-Run subscription software service to the free Debian servers or other free software sources if you don't want to keep paying Linspire for updates. Linspire has great packaging and looks. No free downloads regularly available; restrictive license prohibits sharing outside of immediate family.

(www.linspire.com)

Books that Can Help You Become More Proficient with Linux

Point & Click Linux! is a starting place. If you want to learn more about Linux, either for your own use or in a professional capacity as a programmer or systems administrator, these five titles can help:

Moving to Linux: Kiss the Blue Screen of Death Goodbye
by Marcel Gagne, ISBN 0321159985
If *Point & Click Linux!* is your first Linux book, *Moving to Linux* might be a good second one. It gives you installation instructions for distributions besides MEPIS, plus it'll walk you through a slightly group of applications and give you a larger dose of command line instructions.

Running Linux, 4th Edition
by Matt Welsh, et al, ISBN 0596002726
This book is "the" classic guide to the Linux command line; you'll find it on many professional sysadmins' bookshelves. You may not need this book if you're only running a single home or home office computer, but if you have professional Linux aspirations or want to start building a Linux network for your own home or office, you'll want to have a copy around.

A Practical Guide to Red Hat Linux: Fedora Core and Red Hat Enterprise Linux
By Mark G. Sobell, 0131470248
A comprehensive book aimed at new Linux power users and system and network administrators. Includes the full Fedora Core 2 release on 4 CDs. Good study material if you plan to use Linux professionally, especially because Red Hat is the most popular Linux distribution in corporate server rooms.

The Linux Cookbook
By Michael Stutz, ISBN 1886411484
Shows you how to do many things with Linux through the command line, but instead of just indexing single commands it walks you through entire processes in a recipe-like fashion. This is a fine way to not only become command line-literate but to get in the habit of actually using the command line to do things.

Beginning Linux Programming, 3rd Edition
By Neil Matthews and Richard Stones, ISBN 0764544977
This book assumes you have at least some C or C++ experience and have installed Linux at least a time or two. Buy it if you're ready to start programming in or for Linux. It's one of the best basic guides for programmers who want to start working with Linux.

Appendix C

About MEPIS and the *SimplyMEPIS* CD

COPYRIGHTS AND TRADEMARKS

SimplyMEPIS is a collective work under US copyright law.
Copyright (c) 2003-4 by:
MEPIS LLC
714 Venture Dr., Suite 119
Morgantown, WV 26508
http://www.mepis.org
info@mepis.org

MEPIS, *SimplyMEPIS*, and the MEPIS logo are marks of MEPIS LLC. Unauthorized commercial reuse of the MEPIS names and logos is prohibited. Linux is a registered trademark of Linus Torvalds.

WARRANTY

SimplyMEPIS is provided "AS-IS" without warranty of any kind, either expressed or implied, including, but not limited to, the implied warranties of merchantability, non-infringement, and fitness for a particular purpose.

USER LICENSE

Subject to trademark use limitations set forth herein, MEPIS LLC grants you a license in the collective work pursuant to the GNU General Public License, Version 2, June 1991.

SimplyMEPIS is a Linux operating system consisting of hundreds of individual software components that were individually written and copyrighted. Each program has its own applicable end user license agreement. Most of the programs are licensed pursuant to an open source EULA that permits you to copy, modify, and redistribute the software, in both source code and binary code forms. Nothing in this license limits your rights under, or grants you rights that supersede, theimplyMEPIS terms of any applicable EULA.

ATTENTION US GOVERNMENT USERS

The US Government's rights in this software and accompanying documentation are only as set forth herein, in accordance with 48 CFR 227.7201 through 227.7202-4 and 48 CFR 2.101 and 12.212.

EXPORT

SimplyMEPIS is a publicly available collection of software that contains unmodified publicly available Open Source encryption source code which, together with object code resulting from the compiling of publicly available source code, has been previously cleared for export from the United States under License Exception "TSU" pursuant to EAR Section 740.13(e). Said source code and object code is publicly available at several web sites including `ftp://mirror.mcs.anl.gov/pub/`

The knowing export or re-export of cryptographic software and technology to nationals of Cuba, Iran, Iraq, Libya, North Korea and Sudan is prohibited by US Law.

This legal notice applies to cryptographic software only. More detailed information is available at `http://www.bxa.doc.gov/`

SPECIAL RECOGNITION

SimplyMEPIS and MEPIS Linux stand on the shoulders of the excellent and committed Debian Gnu/Linux community. Without their hard work, MEPIS and other Debian based versions/distributions of Linux would not be possible.

MEPIS is supported by people like you. Some help others at the Forum, or translate help files into different languages, or make suggestions, or work on special projects. Others purchase one or more registrations and download subscriptions of MEPIS Linux. We hope you will join us at Team MEPIS in whatever way is most satisfying for you.

SPECIAL OFFER FOR 'POINT AND CLICK LINUX' READERS

Register your copy of MEPIS and download the latest version of MEPIS free. You'll also get a free 30-day MEPIS Premium subscription that gives you access to over 1000 additional software packages for MEPIS.

(If you don't have a high-speed Internet connection you can have the latest version of MEPIS and additional MEPIS software shipped to you on CDs for a small additional charge.)

To take advantage of this offer, go to `http://store.mepis.com` and enter code *4PH*.

Index

commands

Q – R

S

Get a One Month MEPIS Subscription
FREE!
(normally $10)

MEPIS wants you to have **the latest version of SimplyMEPIS**. As a reader of this book you are entitled to a **special offer**. Visit the MEPIS Web site to register your copy of SimplyMEPIS or use the mail-in coupon below, and you will receive a one month **trial subscription** to the **MEPIS Premium Download Site. This will give you access to all the latest MEPIS-tested software and the latest security updates.** U.S. and Canadian residents also have the choice of receiving the **latest SimplyMEPIS on CD** for a shipping charge of $4.95.

MEPIS Registration and Special Offer Form

MEPIS LLC   **Coupon Code: 4PH**
714 Venture Dr. Suite 119
Morgantown WV 26508
www.mepis.org

I hereby register SimplyMEPIS 2004 for my _____ computer.

___Send the latest SimplyMEPIS CD to my registration address below. I have enclosed $4.95 for shipping and handling. (US and Canada only)

___I like SimplyMEPIS! Enclosed is $_____ to help pay for the further development of SimplyMEPIS.

Registration Name_____

Company_____

Address_____

City_____ State_____ Zip_____

Phone_____ Email_____

___Do not contact me with Special Offers and/or MEPIS News

Because we respect your privacy, we pledge to never sell, rent, or give your personal information to any other organization.

informIT

www.informit.com

YOUR GUIDE TO IT REFERENCE

Articles

Keep your edge with thousands of free articles, in-depth features, interviews, and IT reference recommendations – all written by experts you know and trust.

Online Books

Answers in an instant from **InformIT Online Book's** 600+ fully searchable on line books. For a limited time, you can get your first 14 days **free**.

Catalog

Review online sample chapters, author biographies and customer rankings and choose exactly the right book from a selection of over 5,000 titles.

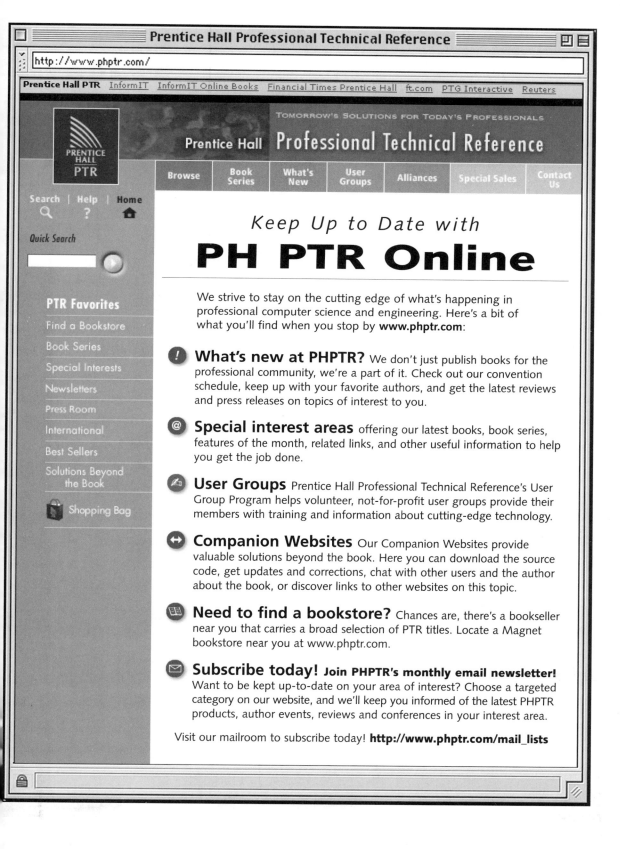